RONALD REAGAN
★ AND HIS RANCH ★
THE WESTERN WHITE HOUSE: 1981 – 1989

RONALD REAGAN
★ AND HIS RANCH ★
THE WESTERN WHITE HOUSE: 1981–1989

BY PETER HANNAFORD

Images From the Past
Bennington, Vermont

1 2 3 4 5 6 7 8 9 10 XXX 10 09 08 07 06 05 04 03 02

First edition

Library of Congress Cataloging-in-Publication Data

Hannaford, Peter.
    Ronald Reagan and his ranch : the western White House, 1981-89 / by Peter Hannaford.
        p. cm.
Includes bibliographical references and index.
    ISBN 1-884592-38-4
1. Reagan, Ronald–Homes and haunts–California–Santa Barbara Region. 2. Rancho del Cielo (Calif.)3. Presidents–United States–Biography. 4. Santa Barbara Region (Calif.)–Biography. I. Title.
E877.2 .H355 2002
979.4'91–dc21

                                    2002005690

Copyright 2002 Peter Hannaford
Published by Images from the Past, Inc.
P.O. Box 137, Bennington, Vermont 05201
www.imagesfromthepast.com
Tordis Ilg Isselhardt, Publisher

Printed in Hong Kong

Design and Production: Ron Toelke Associates, Chatham, NY
Printer: RAAND Print Specialties, Albany, NY

This book is dedicated to
William Wilson, who introduced
Ronald Reagan to the ranch,
the late Willard "Barney" Barnett,
and Dennis LeBlanc, who helped
make it into Rancho del Cielo,
and to Nancy Reagan,
who made it "home."

TABLE OF CONTENTS

Introduction   vii

Chapter One — PRESIDENTIAL RETREATS   1

Chapter Two — FROM 1769-1974   15

Chapter Three — THE RANCH SEARCH   27

Chapter Four — ELBOW GREASE   33

Chapter Five — WELCOME TO RANCHO DEL CIELO   47

Chapter Six — SAFE AND SOUND   57

Chapter Seven — WESTERN WHITE HOUSE DAYS   65

Chapter Eight — STOP THE PRESSES?   81

Chapter Ten — AFTER THE WHITE HOUSE YEARS   93

Post Script   103

Bibliography   105

Index   109

Picture Sources   115

ACKNOWLEDGMENTS

My thanks go to Ron Robinson, president of the Young America's Foundation, and to Floyd Brown, executive director of the Reagan Ranch, for their time and for making both the time and knowledge of their staff available to me. In particular, I am grateful to Marilyn Fisher, curator of the ranch, and to Andrew Coffin.

Joanne Drake, President Reagan's current chief of staff, was very helpful in verifying dates and other facts, and Eric Hvolboll was generous with his extensive knowledge of Santa Barbara County history.

I thank the following for giving generously of their time and recollections in extensive interviews: Nancy Reagan, John Barletta, Lou Cannon, William P. Clark, Dennis LeBlanc, Edwin Meese III, Bill Plante, William Wilson, and Susan Zirinsky.

I am also grateful to the following for their time and assistance: Bess Abell, Richard V. Allen, Martin Anderson, Rosalie Cornelius, John Crockett of the Santa Ynez Valley Historical Association, Sam Donaldson, Kenneth Duberstein, Paul Laxalt, Harry O'Connor, John McCaslin, Ronald Reagan Presidential Library Archivist Cate Sewell, and Margarita Villa.

Last, but not least, my thanks go to Jim Redhage, who first suggested the idea of doing this book; to my publisher, Tordis Ilg Isselhardt, president of Images from the Past, for her lively support of this project; and to my wife, Irene, who has been an inspiration for all my books and who is also an excellent transcriber of interview tapes and spotter of typographical errors in manuscripts.

Rancho del Cielo can make you feel as if you are on a cloud...
—Ronald Reagan

Ronald and Nancy Reagan purchased Tip Top Ranch in Santa Barbara County, California, on November 13, 1974. They renamed it *Rancho del Cielo*—Ranch in the Sky or Sky Ranch.

It lies nearly twenty-seven miles north of Santa Barbara, up a narrow, steep road that snakes its way through Refugio Canyon from the Pacific Coast Highway. On the flat, the road passes lemon and avocado groves. As it rises, it fords several creeks, which are usually dry, crosses two cattle guards, and passes by several dwellings under a canopy of oaks. Once above the woods, it twists and curves its way up the mountainside. If you pass the gate to Rancho del Cielo, the road will take you all the way over the mountain and down to the Santa Ynez Valley.

The main ranch house is at an elevation of 2239 feet above sea level in the Santa Ynez Mountains. The ranch's highest point is Lookout Mountain, at 2587 feet. From a high point on the ranch you can see the Pacific Ocean on one side dotted with the Channel Islands and, on the other, the Santa Ynez Valley.

Gradually, the ranch and its neighbors have become surrounded by the Los Padres National Forest. Coincidentally, the chief ranger for the national forest, in President Theodore Roosevelt's time, was the grandfather of William P. Clark who became Reagan's gubernatorial chief of staff, then a state Supreme Court justice, and later President Reagan's National Security Adviser and Secretary of the Interior.

The ranch consists of 688 acres of pasture, coastal oaks, madrone, dense chaparral and other scrub, and riding trails. The core of the main house is an adobe cottage, which dates from the 1870s. The Reagans converted a wrap-around screen porch into part of the building, creating an L-shaped living-dining-recreation room. In addition, the house has a master bedroom and bath, a maid's room and bath, kitchen, bar, and a den. It is 1500 square feet in all. The house is heated only by fireplaces in the living room and den.

Next to the main house is a two-bedroom guest cottage built by the Reagans in the early 1980s. Next to it is another small building, which is actually a travel trailer, artfully disguised as a trim, small guest facility.

On a rise above the main house and the guest quarters are the Tack Barn, housing the tack room, a workshop area, President's Reagan's blue jeep, and his drive-yourself lawn mower, complete with the Presidential seal. Nearby are the caretaker's cottage and on rises above are the hay barn/stable and a prefabricated metal building, now empty, which housed the Secret Service command center during the Reagan presidency. Other special facilities, such as the helicopter pad, installed during President Reagan's White House years, were removed when he retired from office in 1989.

At the time the Reagans purchased the ranch, I was Assistant to the Governor and Director of Public Affairs in Sacramento. Michael K. Deaver, Assistant to the Governor and Director of Administration, and I had proposed to provide the Reagans management and administration of their public program after he left office. They agreed. In the first week of January 1975, Deaver & Hannaford, Inc., opened its doors in Los Angeles, with by-then-former Governor Reagan's private office inside our suite. We had assembled a team from the Governor's Office staff to work with us in support of the Reagans' activities. As it turned out, this arrangement would last five years, until Ronald Reagan's successful 1980 presidential campaign. Rancho del Cielo was to be a regular part of the Reagans' lives during all that time—and for many years after.

This, then, is the story of the Reagans' ranch; its history; how it fits into the succession of presidential retreats over 200 years; how the Reagans acquired it and made it into a home of their own; and the events and people it witnessed from January 1981 to January 1989, when it served as the Western White House. Reagan never called it that, according to Lou Cannon, the *Washington Post* correspondent who covered virtually all of Reagan's political career. Cannon noted, "He once said to me, 'There's only one White House, and that's in Washington, D.C.'"

In effect, however, the major functions of the White House go wherever the president goes—in this case to Rancho del Cielo. The press who covered Reagan and the public who followed what he was doing called it the Western White House, and so it was.

—Peter Hannaford
Mattole Valley, California
April 2002

American presidents, like their fellow citizens, savor a complete change from their daily routine now and then. While they travel around the world at a pace unimaginable even fifty years ago, hopping across the Atlantic for a one-day meeting with a head of state is not really a change of scene. The schedule is tightly arranged and scripted. The president sees fleeting scenes from his limousine, from the interior of Air Force One, and from the rooms in which his meetings are conducted. At home or abroad, the president must be "on" every waking moment, preparing for or conducting official business.

A modern-day president may take a series of short vacations at his own retreat. Or, if he doesn't have one, as was the case with Bill Clinton, he will take a longer summer vacation at a place owned by friends. In either case, the White House staff and press corps go where the president goes.

A personal retreat has several advantages. Like the summer cottages owned by millions of Americans, it is familiar and comfortable. You know where everything is. A president's personal retreat also has the security and communications trappings of the presidency built in, so planning a visit—even a short one—is less complicated than planning a vacation at say a remote mountain lake or a beach front villa.

THE FIRST PRESIDENTIAL RETREAT

These were not considerations when Thomas Jefferson built the first presidential retreat, Poplar Forest. He conceived and designed it in 1806 and then built it over the next dozen years on his 4,000-acre plantation, which was six-and-a-half miles from Lynchburg, Virginia. It was about sixty miles from his principal residence, Monticello, near Charlottesville. At Poplar Forest Jefferson could contemplate the state of the nation, work on his inventions, and pursue his interest in architecture.

Given the constraints of travel at that time, for most other early presidents their homes were their retreats. George Washington's retreat was his beloved Mount Vernon, on the Virginia shore of the Potomac River, thirteen miles southeast of what is now Washington, D.C. For several years during the Revolutionary War, Washington did not get to visit his home even once, although he sent frequent detailed instructions back to his farm manager, as well as letters to his wife, Martha, whom he affectionately called "Patsy." During Washington's Presidency, the capitol was in Philadelphia; nevertheless, with the exception of those few years, he had managed to make frequent sojourns home, although none of his visits were as long as those taken by his successor, John Adams.

Adams initiated the concept of a "Summer White House" (although the official presidential residence in Washington—first occupied by Adams in 1800—did not acquire the name "White House" until years later). In 1797, the first year of his Presidency, Adams left Philadelphia nine days after Congress recessed, on July 19, for his farm, Peacefield, in Quincy, Massachusetts. *The Aurora,* a rabid anti-Federalist newspaper, excoriated Adams for leaving the capital at a time when public opinion was "exceedingly agitated." Despite the criticism, it was a quiet summer. Adams conducted presidential business from Peacefield until the first week in October, when he returned to Philadelphia.

The next summer, his removal of the presidential residence to Quincy lasted even longer. David McCullough in his biography, *John Adams,* says, "There was precious little peace at Peacefield in the summer of 1798." One reason was that that summer Adams's wife, Abigail, sustained a serious illness. She fortunately recovered. The following year, 1799, Adams spent seven consecutive months in Quincy. His critics were more vociferous than ever, but Adams carried out his duties at Peacefield from March through September, in part perhaps motivated to avoid the Yellow Fever scare that hit Philadelphia every summer and fall. By his final year in office, 1800, the capitol had moved to Washington. The President's House was still being built and Adams was in a campaign for reelection. He left for Quincy on June 14 and headed back to Washington only four months later, on October 13.

Adams's immediate successors, Jefferson, James Madison, and James Monroe had shorter distances to travel to get home, as they were all Virginians. Jefferson, of course, had Monticello and later his Poplar Forest retreat. Madison retreated to his country estate, Montpelier, in Orange County. Monroe first had Ash Lawn, the home designed for him by Jefferson on a 600-acre estate, then Oak Hill, near Leesburg, Virginia, also designed by Jefferson.

Most of the subsequent century presidents had spacious homes that had either long been in their families or were acquired by them as their careers advanced where they went for occasional vacations. Lincoln was a notable exception. He made the Soldiers' Home, in the heights above Washington, his Summer White House. With the Civil War going on, he could not travel far, and the higher elevation above the city provided cooling breezes and relief from the humidity that plagued the capital in the summer.

TWENTIETH–CENTURY PATTERNS

In the twentieth century, Theodore Roosevelt renewed John Adams's dedication to a Summer White House. During the summers between 1901-09 he conducted presidential business in the summer from Sagamore Hill, his large home that overlooked Oyster Bay on Long Island's north shore. There, on the wide porch that wrapped around the south and west sides of the house, he conducted his daily affairs. At Sagamore Hill he received notice that he had been nominated for Governor of New York (1898), Vice President (1900), and President (1904). For Roosevelt, Oyster Bay evoked the happy summers of his childhood.

In 1884, following the death of his first wife and his mother, Roosevelt purchased two cattle ranches on the Missouri River in the Dakota Territory. There he lived the strenuous life of a cowboy for three years, tending cattle and hunting. He is the only presidential rancher prior to Lyndon Johnson and Ronald Reagan, although his ranching but not his love of the outdoor life ended before he became President.

Woodrow Wilson, when he was President, had no home other than the White House. During his first summer as President, in 1913, his wife, Ellen, who was an accomplished painter, and their daughters went to an artists' colony, Haarlachen, in Cornish, New Hampshire. Wilson joined them for eight days in July, making the place a brief Summer White House. Ellen died the following summer. In other years, he spent time in Seagirt, New Jersey, and Pass Christian, Mississippi. He had a car and a staff of two—his secretary and a stenographer—on hand.

Wilson's successor, Warren Harding, who died at the beginning of his thirtieth month in office, liked to spend weekends on the presidential yacht, on railroad excursions, or with friends in the country. In July 1921, his first summer in office, he joined an annual retreat called "Nature's Laboratory," which was organized by Harvey Firestone, Henry Ford, and Thomas Edison on wooded property owned by Firestone in rural Maryland. "Nature's Laboratory" was started several years before by naturalist John Burroughs as a rustic experience, but by the time Harding joined it, it required fifty cars to transport its participants to their rustic retreat. There was a radio car with a cipher so that Harding could keep in touch with the State Department. Harding most enjoyed chopping wood and taking walks with his famous fellow-campers.

The following year, Harding, with his wife, Florence, General John Pershing, and a large entourage, drove by motorcade from Washington to Marion, Ohio, to celebrate the centennial of the Hardings' hometown.

By 1923, worried about emerging scandals in the administration in addition to his declining popularity, Harding decided to take a long rail trip through the American West. This was intended to rally support for a 1924 reelection bid. On June 20, the Hardings left a very humid Washington in a ten-car train. He waved to the crowd from the platform of his personal car, the Superb, at the end of the train. He was not to see Washington again. Six weeks later, in San Francisco, he died.

At that time, August 2, 1923, Vice President Calvin Coolidge was vacationing with his family at his father's farm in Plymouth Notch, Vermont. His father, a notary public, administered the presidential oath of office by the light of a kerosene lantern in his home late that night.

The next August, that farm home became Coolidge's Summer White House. He and his wife, Grace, and son, John, were accompanied by his Secretary (the term for earlier-day chiefs of staff), a physician, a stenographer, two clerks, and twelve newspaper reporters. In addition, there was a contingent of eighteen Secret Service agents, the most assigned to a presidential Summer White House up to that time. Business was conducted in the second floor hall above the village store, a hall that was usually the site of dances and Grange dinners. Wood planks on sawhorses served as desks and telephone and telegraph lines were specially installed so the president and his staff could stay in contact with Washington.

For his next four years in office, Coolidge took his summer breaks at Swampscott, on the Massachusetts shore; the Adirondack Mountains in New York; the Black Hills of South Dakota; and Wisconsin. During these sojourns he indulged in his favorite pastime, fishing, of which he said, "the unhurried silence, the refreshing leisure are a stimulation to the body and a benediction to the soul."

During 1929, his first year in office, Herbert Hoover, Coolidge's successor, had a retreat built in Virginia's Blue Ridge Mountains, one hundred miles southwest of Washington. Camp Rapidan was paid for by the Hoovers. On its 164 acres were several cabins and a school. There was a large outdoor stone fireplace for campfires, extensive hiking trails, and man-made trout pools. Among the Hoovers' guests were British Prime Minister Ramsay MacDonald and Charles and Anne Lindbergh. Hoover's Secretary, Ted Joslin, was a regular at the retreat, as were the White House physician and the Secretary of the Interior, Ray Lyman Wilbur. Mrs. Hoover even held a number of Girl Scout events at Camp Rapidan. When Hoover left office, he donated the camp to the Shenandoah National Park for use by future presidents.

Franklin D. Roosevelt preferred a retreat closer to Washington, so the government-built-and-owned compound called "Shangri-la" was created in the late 1930s in the Catoctin Mountains of Maryland, about fifty miles northwest of Washington. President Dwight D. Eisenhower renamed the site Camp David after his grandson, and Camp David it has been ever since.

Roosevelt also had two other retreats. One was at Warm Springs, Georgia. He found the waters there to have therapeutic effects on his legs, which had been crippled by polio. He had a small cottage built for himself on the grounds. He also had a small house built on family property at Hyde Park, New York, on the Hudson River.

In August 1946, a year and a half after he took office following

Roosevelt's death, Harry Truman made the presidential yacht, the *Williamsburg,* his retreat. He took several poker-playing friends down the Potomac River and out the Chesapeake Bay, up the Atlantic coast to New England, playing poker—which was said to be Truman's favorite form of relaxation—all the way. He later took many short poker party cruises on the *Williamsburg.* He also took respites at the family home in Independence, Missouri, but the Naval Station at Key West, Florida became "The Little White House" for many of his sojourns. On one retreat there, he heard his daughter, Margaret, on the radio, as she made her singing debut with the Detroit Symphony Orchestra. And it was there that he donned brightly patterned, tails-out Hawaiian shirts for his daily walks around the perimeter of the base. Truman holds the record for the least visits to the official presidential retreat that became Camp David in Eisenhower's time: nine, in nearly eight years. Reagan, by contrast, visited Camp David 187 times, restoring the horse trails that had been built for John F. Kennedy.

Eisenhower purchased a farm near Gettysburg, Pennsylvania, during his presidency and used it as a retreat, and on leaving office, he retired to the farm.

Kennedy used his house in the family compound at Hyannisport, Massachusetts, at the base of Cape Cod, as his retreat.

LBJ—ANOTHER RANCHER

Lyndon Johnson was the first president to have a ranch as his retreat. He and his wife, Lady Bird, had purchased it from an aunt of his during his days in the Senate. On the Pedernales River, not many miles from Johnson's birthplace, the LBJ Ranch was the site of constant activity during Johnson's presidency. Nestled in the hills about an hour's drive from Austin, the ranch had its own airstrip, and LBJ would usually arrive and leave on an Air Force Lockheed Jet Star. The ranch, approximately 400 acres in size, had cattle, but more importantly, it served as an extension of the White House. Johnson gathered around him staff, cabinet members, and advisors. The first foreign leader to call on him at the ranch after he became president was Ludwig Erhard, Chancellor of West Germany. Israeli and Mexican leaders followed. One time the Johnsons entertained the ambassadors from all the Latin American countries with a barbecue.

The main LBJ Ranch house had several guest rooms. In addition, the Guest House had four double bedrooms and, within walking distance, the Cedar House had another three.

Johnson had an unusual "guest book" at the ranch. After he suffered a heart attack in 1955, when he was in the Senate, guests signed their names in blocks of wet cement, thus creating permanent "get-well" cards. From then on, all the visitors to the LBJ Ranch signed in this way, and the ranch pathways and trails became marked by these "signature" blocks.

Richard Nixon initially used his home at Key Biscayne, Florida for his presidential retreat. Later, he purchased Casa Pacifica at the edge of the ocean, south of San Clemente, in Orange County, Southern California. This served as the Summer White House several times during his years in office and, upon resigning in August 1974, was the home to which he retired.

Gerald Ford, the thirty-eighth president, a skiing enthusiast, had a vacation home at Vail, Colorado, which he also used for summer visits. His other home, in Rancho Mirage, California, near Palm Springs, became a winter-spring retreat.

Jimmy Carter's retreat and Summer White House was his home in Plains, Georgia. One major newspaper correspondent who was assigned to cover President Carter on a vacation sojourn in Plains described his time as "the longest two weeks I have ever spent."

By the time he was inaugurated, in January 1981, Ronald Reagan had owned Rancho del Cielo for over five years. The major remodeling had been finished. The ranch was there to enjoy, and he did, whenever he could arrange it. In all, he spent 364 days at the ranch during his eight-year presidency—an average of forty-five days a year, usually split between a spring sojourn, two weeks or so in late summer, a Thanks-giving retreat, and occasional other visits. Reagan visited the ranch some forty times during his presidency. Like several of his predecessors and successors, he also came to love the quietude of Camp David on weekends when it was impractical to leave the Washington, D.C. area.

George Bush's retreat—the family compound at Walker's Point, near Kennebunkport, Maine—became his Summer White House, in addition to being the site of many other shorter visits during the year. He fished, and piloted his "cigarette" speedboat (so named for its straight, thin shape) in the coastal waters.

Bill Clinton owned no home during his presidency, so summer vacations and golfing weekends were held at the retreat homes of friends. It is said that he consulted public opinion polls before deciding each year where he and his family would vacation.

George W. Bush, like Ronald Reagan and Lyndon Johnson, has a ranch he loves, near Crawford, Texas. He had purchased the ranch prior to his being elected, like Reagan's Rancho del Cielo, and the ranch was more-or-less automatically suited for any short retreats, as well as for the Summer White House in August 2001. Bush was criticized by some in the press for planning to spend a month there—possibly because they feared being detailed to duty in tiny Crawford. One public opinion poll indicated that a majority of Americans thought he should be at the White House instead, so his staff scheduled a variety of one-day events in various parts of the country during his "ranch month."

With one exception, Ronald Reagan's sojourns at Rancho del Cielo were unbroken once he got there.

Mount Vernon, home of first president George Washington, in Virginia.

2
FROM 1769 TO 1974

It was August. An ocean breeze cut the heat of the sun, a welcome relief after all the days of riding and marching from San Diego. This site would make a good town, mission, even garrisoned presidio; already there were many natives settled here. It would come to be called Santa Barbara.

Don Gaspar de Portola, recently named Governor of Baja California, was carrying out the dream of his superior, José de Galvez, the *visitador-general* of New Spain. Ever since he arrived in Mexico in 1765, Galvez was intent on colonizing Alta California, which was thus far only nominally Spanish. His plan was to establish a series of missions with accompanying towns or *pueblos* and, in some locations, forts or *presidios*.

Galvez's plan called for Portola to take an expedition north from Baja California north to San Diego, then up to Monterey. Portola assembled a group of mestizo soldiers. Under him were three men who were destined to play roles in the development of Alta California in later years. Comandante Fernando Rivera y Moncad and Lieutenant Pedro Fages were to become governors of the province, Sergeant José Francisco de Ortega, founded the Santa Barbara presidio (in 1782) and became *comandante* of the presidio at San Diego and also *comandante* at Monterey. He ended thirty years of service to the Spanish crown as *comandante* of the royal garrison at Loreto in Baja California.

In early 1769, Portola's expedition—consisting of three ships and two land parties—set out from Mexico for San Diego. By August, one of the land expeditions had reached the shore of an indentation in the coast, a site that was to become Santa Barbara. They continued by horseback and on foot to Monterey, following the coastal plain west of Santa Barbara, the Santa Ynez Mountains were a backdrop to their right. About twenty-five miles west of Santa Barbara, they passed a canyon that came to be known as *El Refugio*—the refuge. Above them, at an elevation of 2,200 feet in a broad bowl in the mountains was the land that 205 years later would become Ronald Reagan's Rancho del Cielo.

Father Juan Crespi, the priest who accompanied the expedition, wrote of the coastal land, "The country along the road is extremely delightful, abounding in pasture and covered with oaks, willows, and other trees, giving signs of its being very fertile land, capable of producing whatever one might wish to plant."

The party turned inland a few miles further on, at Gaviota Pass or Point Conception, then marched north to Monterey by a route that was very close to what would become the main route from Monterey to San Diego, *El Camino Real,* the Royal Road, today less poetically known as U.S. Highway 101. Sergeant Ortega was the expedition's chief scout, setting the party's route and locating camp sites and water sources to mark the end of each day's march. He was the first of the expedition, thus the first Spaniard (and possibly the first European) to discover San Francisco Bay.

The Spanish lost no time following through on Portola's expedition. The Franciscans, under Father Junipero Serra and later Father Fermin Lasuén, built and staffed twenty-one missions between San

Diego and Sonoma, which lies north of San Francisco. The missions were a day's march apart and had substantial land holdings, ostensibly in trust for the local Indians. Towns built up around most of them. Presidios were established at four locations: San Diego, Santa Barbara, Monterey, and San Francisco. The infrastructure that was developed was intended to discourage other foreigners with designs on California and to keep the local Indians under control of the mission system.

One often hears the term "Spanish land grant" in connection with California's history, but in fact, the number of land concessions, not actual grants, made in California under Spanish rule was fewer than two dozen. It was not until Mexico declared its independence from Spain in 1822 that the number of land concessions substantially increased. For example, from the time the missions were secularized in 1833 until the American occupation of California in 1846, some 700 land "grants" were issued to private owners.

THE ORTEGA RANCH

During the Spanish era there was only one land concession issued in what would become Santa Barbara County. That one was given to José Francisco de Ortega—Portola's scout—for the 26,529 acres of Rancho Nuestra Senora del Refugio. The exact date of this concession is not known; however, records show that the Ortegas settled at Refugio in 1794. Their ranch covered a stretch of eighteen miles of the same coastal terrace at the base of the Santa Ynez Mountains where Sergeant Ortega had trod with the Portola expedition, below the mountain bowl that would one day be Ronald Reagan's ranch.

The Ortega hacienda was built on a knoll a mile up Refugio Canyon from the coastal plain. They soon grew wheat and tree fruits, produced wine, and pastured cattle and horses.

In 1804, José María Ortega, son of José Francisco, petitioned the governor for the legal title to the Refugio ranch, but the padres of Mission Santa Barbara objected on the grounds that the original concession was given with the condition that the Ortegas might one day need to give up the land so that the mission's nearly 3000 neophytes might use it to produce food for themselves. The padres argued that the mission's own lands, stretching southeast from the Refugio ranch to the mission itself, did not have enough water to support the cattle and crops needed for the population. The governor did not respond, leaving the status quo intact.

Again in 1813 and 1817, the Ortegas petitioned for the legal title to the land. Both petitions were denied. In December 1829, the Ortegas sent a new petition to the *comandante* at Santa Barbara. It was ignored until 1834, when José Figueroa became governor and ordered that all the missions become secularized. In July that year, he directed that the Ortegas be granted title to the land. Judicial possession, confirming the boundaries of the ranch, did not follow until 1846, fifty years after the Ortegas had first occupied the land.

SMUGGLERS AND REBELS

Smuggling was a regular coastal activity in the early years of the nineteenth century. Trade with foreign ships was forbidden under Spanish law, yet many manufactured goods were available only from sea-borne traders, mostly from New England. The law made an exception in the case of ships that needed to take on water, food, or medicine or that required repairs, and many American ships moored off the Santa Barbara coast under this guise. A favorite smuggler's anchorage was Refugio Bay, offshore from the Ortega ranch, a short distance, as the crow flies, below the mountain site of the Reagan ranch.

The smugglers would land clothing and a variety of other manu-factured goods and sail away with sea otter and fur seal skins. Occa-sionally, Yankee ships would be seized by the authorities, but it was tacitly understood that their cargo was "necessary," for such goods could not be easily supplied from Mexico.

These were years of political ferment in the South American provinces of the Spanish empire. In 1808 revolts ensued in several of the provinces. Within a few years, insurgents in Buenos Aires, Argentina, were hiring ships to harass Spanish ships and stir up rebellion throughout the colonies.

In October 1818, Santa Barbara was alerted by an American ship that two rebel ships were about to attack the California coast. Their targets were said to be Monterey, the Ortega ranch, which was thought to contain great riches, Santa Barbara, and San Juan Capistrano.

Santa Barbara Comandante José de la Guerra sent a courier to Monterey to warn Governor Solá that the two rebel ships, under a French commander, Hippolyte de Bouchard, had 54 cannons and 280 fighting men between them.

On October 27, the Argentine ships reached Monterey Bay. Bouchard demanded that Solá surrender all of Alta California. Solá refused and the rebels sacked the provincial capital the next day. Governor Solá fled with the archives and sent a courier south to warn Santa Barbara that the rebels were on their way.

De la Guerra arranged for the evacuation of women, elderly men, children, and the Santa Barbara Mission's valuables. In the rain, most of the evacuees went over the Santa Ynez Mountains via the Ortega ranch and Refugio Pass (passing close by the Reagan ranch) to Santa Ynez.

The privateers anchored in Refugio Bay on December 2. Before they did, Sergeant José María Ortega, son of José Francisco, sent three brass-studded chests to the family ranch from the presidio in Santa Barbara. He instructed his relatives to pack up all their silks, silver, gold, pearls, and other valuables and leave Refugio Ranch without delay for Santa Ynez Mission. Thus, Bouchard and his men found the ranch deserted. Furious, they burned buildings, tore up the vineyard, and slaughtered every animal they could find.

A platoon of Spanish soldiers reached the Refugio ranch too late to stop the rampage; however, they did capture three of Bouchard's men. Comandante de la Guerra thwarted Bouchard's intention to sack Santa Barbara by riding his small military contingent around and around a low hill, giving the rebels the impression that he had hundreds of soldiers. Later, he traded the rebel prisoners for Bouchard's single hostage and the rebels sailed away.

The Bear Flag Revolt

In December 1846, another milestone in California's history occurred not far from the mountain that contained the future Reagan ranch. Following the Bear Flag Revolt, which had been staged in Sonoma by American settlers to foment support for the annexation of California by the United States, John C. Fremont led his army of sixty men south. Although his arrival in California in 1845 was ostensibly for the purpose of scientific exploration, his real purpose was to assist in the movement to acquire California for the United States.

On a wet Christmas Day in 1846, Fremont crossed through San Marcos Pass, north of Santa Barbara. Two days later, he marched into the town and took control of it while most of its inhabitants were in church.

A little over thirteen months later, on February 2, 1848, following the Mexican War, the United States acquired California under the terms of the Treaty of Guadalupe Hidalgo.

The treaty called for the protection of land titles held by Mexican citizens; however, in 1851, Congress passed a law placing the burden of proof of ownership on the landholders, not on the American newcomers who were challenging them. Unfamiliar with the American legal system and, in many cases, the English language, many *Californios,* as they were called, had to mortgage or sell their property to pay the legal costs of defending their titles. It was a dark chapter in the Americanization of California.

By 1860, the old *ranchero* system was fractured; however, the Ortega family held on to their land longer than most—for another two decades. Their huge ranch, at the base of the mountains where Ronald Reagan would one day have Rancho del Cielo, was gradually sold off by the Ortega family members in eight parcels, the last one sold in 1880. This was not quite the end of the Ortega connection; the last family member left the property ninety years later, in the 1970s.

SETTLERS IN THE MOUNTAINS

Meanwhile, there was activity in the mountains above the coastal plain. Much of the terrain was covered in brush and otherwise unsuitable for grazing animals; however, some land was cleared, and, gradually, during the last half of the nineteenth century ranchers began to settle on the land. This was government land, successively Spanish, Mexican, and then American. It was not until August 1, 1898 that the first title was issued for the initial 160 acres of what was to become the Reagan ranch. José Jesús Pico obtained the title from the U.S. Government under the 1862 Homestead Act. It is likely that José and Juana Pico actually lived on the property from 1870, and perhaps earlier, for the small adobe ranch house is said to have been built in 1871.

José had moved north from Mexico and had worked on other ranches in the area before settling at what was to become Rancho del Cielo. Here he grew beans, corn, potatoes, tomatoes, watermelons, and enough grapes to produce as much as 900 gallons of wine a year.

He also raised horses, cattle, chickens, and hogs.

José and Juana's son Edward was born on the ranch on April 17, 1896, before they acquired their homestead title. He spent his youth on the ranch and was schooled there.

Subsequent owners up to the eve of World War II included José Jesús Romero, Belisanio Robles, Virginia Angulo, Margaret Combetto, Natale Bazzi, Arlangelo (sic) and Luigi Goggia, and Charles and Mary Gandolio. In 1941, Santa Barbara County Surveyor Frank Flournoy bought the property for $6,000. He named it Tip Top Ranch.

Near the ranch were several sandstone quarries, which supplied the stone for many of the major buildings of Santa Barbara. A number of stonecutters from Italy, who came over to work the sandstone, settled on nearby ranches. The Rennie ranch, just east of the Reagan ranch, is the only one in the area still owned by the family that first settled it. Mrs. Rennie is a descendant of the Goggia family, the original settlers on that property.

On April 12, 1955, the core of what was to become Rancho del Cielo was sold to rancher Raymond Cornelius and his wife, Rosalie. They added four parcels to their holdings between then and 1970, in swaps with the U.S. Forest Service for land the Cornelius family owned elsewhere in California and which the U.S.F.S. wished to acquire. Over nearly twenty years, their holdings grew to 2000 acres. They grazed up to 400 cattle on the ranch at any one time.

Although they had a resident foreman on the ranch, the Cornelius's spent quite a lot of time there, living in the small adobe. According to Rosalie Cornelius, "There was always plenty to do, such as fixing fences and roads." Friends were often invited to enjoy the beauty and peacefulness of the site. The children would swim and boat in the small lake until it dried late in the summer.

They sold two parcels—one of 1000 acres and one of a little over 300 acres—before selling the final 688 acres to the Reagans on November 13, 1974. This land, which would become Rancho del Cielo, had been silent witness to the colonization of California by Spain and Mexico, and to its acquisition by the United States. Before long, it would become the site of the Western White House.

3
THE RANCH SEARCH

me at the right time. Our daughter was killed in a head-on automobile accident recently near Santa Ynez. We'd been keeping it for her one day. Now, if you want to buy, let us talk.'"

That led to the first visit to the property by the Reagans. Willard "Barney" Barnett, the Governor's driver in Southern California, was a retired California Highway Patrolman. One weekend he drove them from Los Angeles to the Wilson ranch where they met Bill and Betty Wilson and proceeded up Refugio Canyon Road. It was their first time on the increasingly steep, narrow, and twisting road. "Nancy wasn't so sure she was going to like this road," Wilson said, "but Ronnie said, 'Let's keep going,' and we did.

"The way you approached it in those days was over a little hill and into the valley where the little house was located. At that time of the year there was a dirt dam near the house, with some water behind it. Ronnie fell in love with the place immediately—before we got anywhere near the house. As we got closer to it, he said, 'It's absolutely gorgeous here. I love it.' Ray Cornelius was waiting for us up by the house and I said, 'Ronnie, don't talk like that or the price will go up.'" Mrs. Reagan confirms the story and says of the ranch, "My first impression was that it was so beautiful. We'd want to do a lot of work on the little adobe house, but that was part of the charm for both Ronnie and me. There were so many things to do and that appealed to us both. That and the fact the land was so pretty and there were so many trails. I think we decided right then that we wanted to buy it."

Reagan, in his memoirs, *An American Life,* recounts that Ray Cornelius "put us on horses and we took a ride over the place. Well, after that, I was really sold."

Several years later, journalist and Reagan chronicler Lou Cannon recalls Nancy Reagan telling him that her husband had a preference for heights, citing the mountain location of the ranch and, later of the Ronald Reagan Presidential Library, which is also on a peak above Simi Valley in Ventura County.

COMPLETING THE PURCHASE

It took a year to complete the purchase, in part because it took time to sell the Rancho California property. Finally, on November 13, 1974, Tip Top Ranch—as it was called—was theirs. Ronald Reagan, with a little over seven weeks to go before the end of his second term as Governor of California, was itching to get to work on their new ranch. In December, recalls Dennis LeBlanc, a member of the Governor's security detail at the time and soon to be his aide in private life, the Reagans visited the ranch and began planning the work that lay ahead in the new year.

The Reagans had selected their own name for the place: Rancho del Cielo, or "Sky Ranch."

Years later, he would say of it, "From the first day we saw it, Rancho del Cielo cast a spell over us. No place before or since has even given Nancy and me the joy and serenity it does."

On the morning of Thursday, January 2, 1975, Governor Ronald Reagan flew into Sacramento from Los Angeles to spend two final days in his Capitol office. Downtown Sacramento was blanketed by a layer of cold, damp tule fog. He spent much of the day doing "exit" interviews with the news media, reviewing eight years of his work. He was leaving office with high approval ratings, and the state government's finances were in good shape.

The next morning dawned clear and bright. I had occasion to see him about some detail. His corner office looked out over Capitol Park which surrounded the state capitol building, its deep green lawn filled with mature specimen trees. The sight was always a spirit-raiser. He looked up from some papers and out at the park. Smiling, with an arched eyebrow and a mischievous look in his eye, he said, "Let's not leave."

He had good reason to be happy. In addition to completing two terms that were largely successful, new adventures lay ahead. Over the New Year's holiday, President Gerald Ford had called to invite him to join the cabinet. It was flattering, but Reagan had other things in mind. There would be a five-day-a-week radio commentary, a week or so each month on the road giving speeches to civic and political groups, a syndicated newspaper column, and the urgings of fans throughout the country to challenge Ford for the Republican nomination in 1976.

And there was the ranch. Ever since they had purchased it the previous November, he and his wife had been deep in plans for how they wanted to make Rancho del Cielo their personal retreat. He was itching to get to work.

JANUARY 1975: "CIVILIAN" LIFE

On Sunday, January 5, Ronald Reagan's gubernatorial term ended. The next morning, several new chapters in his life began. Michael Deaver and I, both senior assistants to Governor Reagan, had proposed to provide coordination and administration of his program after he left office. He approved of the plan and we formed a new company, Deaver & Hannaford, Inc., and arranged to open for business in Los Angeles on January 6, 1975.

Our new suite of offices on the eighth floor of a building in the Westwood section of Los Angeles included a personal office for Ronald Reagan, a near duplicate of his corner office in the State Capitol. Mrs. Reagan oversaw its decoration. The furnishings in his Capitol office had been his own, and these familiar items were awaiting him. From his new office, instead of the view of the Capitol Park grounds, he looked out to the south to see airplanes landing and taking off a few miles away at Los Angeles International Airport. To the west, on a clear day, he could easily make out Santa Catalina Island, the southernmost of the Channel Islands, about twenty-five miles away. One hundred miles to the north, the upper end of this chain of islands, was just offshore from Rancho del Cielo.

Mike and I had assembled a small team from the Governor's staff to work on the Reagan program. Helene von Damm, his executive secretary in Sacramento, would be our office manager. Nancy Reynolds, who had assisted Mrs. Reagan with her program, would do "advance" work in support of the travel schedule. Dennis LeBlanc, from the security detail, would be the principal advance person and would coordinate security matters. Barney Barnett would continue to be Governor Reagan's driver and aide. Mike and I would provide oversight of the team and coordinate the program. In addition, a group of volunteers from the West Side Republican Women's Club offered to create a correspondence unit to respond to citizen letters, which continued to come in at a steady and heavy rate.

The January Reagan schedule was virtually complete by the time we opened our doors. In my 1983 book, *The Reagans: A Political Portrait*, I wrote, "The governor (we all continued to call him by that title even though he was now a private citizen) was anxious to spend time out of doors remodeling and expanding the small adobe ranch house. Still, the demands of his new schedule that month did not allow as much ranch time as he had hoped.

"There was the newspaper column to get started, a trip back to Sacramento on the twenty-first for the unveiling of the official Reagan portrait in the Capitol building, the first radio taping on the twenty-third and, on the thirtieth, the start of his first lecture tour.

"The Sacramento trip went well. It was a clear, crisp day. The new governor, Jerry Brown, welcomed the Reagans back to the capitol and made a short but gracious speech about Ronald Reagan's tenure in

Sacramento; Reagan gave an equally gracious response. All seemed to enjoy it. The Reagans liked his portrait by Robert Rishell (the same artist who painted the California country scene that hangs in the den at Rancho del Cielo). It shows a smiling, confident Ronald Reagan standing in front of the Capitol, looking as if he had enjoyed every minute of those eight years.

"On the afternoon of the twenty-third, Barney Barnett drove us to Harry O'Connor's Hollywood recording studios. It is doubtful if the intersection of Hollywood and Vine ever lived up to its legendary fame as a place where one could see the mighty of the motion picture business. By the mid-1970s, its fame rested on that durable legend and the fact that it was a gathering place for a fascinating variety of eccentrics. When Ronald Reagan alighted from the car in front of the Taft Building, it took only a minute or two for a crowd of them to gather, greeting him with quips and cheers.

"Up on the eighth floor, Harry O'Connor had prepared a surprise party. His production crew was there, as were Art Linkletter, Jack Webb, Doug Willis of the Associated Press Sacramento bureau, and Sally Cobb, widow of Bob Cobb, founder of the Brown Derby restaurant down the street. Reagan worked through his scripts smoothly and comfortably. We had decided to record three weeks' worth at each taping—fifteen programs in all . . . Every program ended with, 'This is Ronald Reagan. Thanks for listening.'

"No sooner had he finished the last script than Sally Cobb's Brown Derby staff appeared with champagne and hors d'oeuvres. The Reagan daily commentary was thus launched. Initially, O'Connor had signed up nearly 100 stations; it was to grow to more than 350 by early fall that year . . . Copley News Service kicked off the once-a-week Reagan newspaper column the same week."

WORK DAYS AT THE RANCH

Despite all this activity and preparations for Governor Reagan's first speaking tour at the end of the month, he managed to work in several days at the ranch. Dennis LeBlanc and Barney Barnett joined him in what was to become a two-year work pattern.

At a meeting to review the February schedule, Reagan reminded us that he had a lot of work to do at the ranch and to "remember to build some ranch time into that schedule."

The ranch house had an L-shaped aluminum-screened porch around the front. The Reagans planned to close it in to make a combination living room-dining room. They also planned to expand the main bedroom. There was much painting to do, old fences to repair, and new ones to be built.

Ronald Reagan laid the stone patio in front of the ranch house himself, using stones he had found on the property. He also found three large rocks that had been used long before by Chumash Indians for grinding acorns, which he had repositioned by the patio. Later, when Rancho del Cielo became known as the Western White House, the Reagans hung a sign above the patio, featuring a black horse with the address, "1600 Pennsylvania Avenue."

Dennis LeBlanc recalls that Rush Hill, another Reagan aide in Sacramento, had opened an architectural practice in Newport Beach, and Hill ended up redesigning the kitchen. Hill also had a client who manufactured roofing materials, including half-round red Spanish tiles made from fiberglass. Together, Governor Reagan, Dennis, and Barney re-roofed the house, despite some windy days that blew the light-weight tiles about. "Sometimes the three of us would go up and back every day for three days in a row," LeBlanc recalls. "Anne, the Reagans' housekeeper, would pack a lunch for us or we'd stop at a Kentucky Fried Chicken place on the way up."

Nancy Reagan joined the group many times. "The house was a tiny adobe and we did a lot of work on it, but I think that was part of the charm for both Ronnie and me," she recalls. "There were so many things to do and fix up that appealed to both of us." She took on the painting. "I painted the whole thing and we laid the tile [together]. We worked there day and night."

Once the Reagan's bedroom was completed, in late 1976 or early 1977, LeBlanc recalls, the party began staying overnight. "The maid's room and bath off the kitchen had been redecorated, so Anne would usually go up, too, and prepare meals for the group. Barney and I used the little trailer outside the back door."

What had once been a travel trailer had been set permanently behind the house, its wheels no longer showing. Nancy Reagan deco-rated it in light, cheerful colors. "The trailer was not really a guest house, but I made it into a guest room," she described. In the early eighties, during the Reagan presidency, a two-bedroom guest house, with its own parlor, was built between the main house and the trailer.

CREATING LAKE LUCKY

A year-round pond was also on the list of projects for the ranch. Lake Lucky, as it came to be called, was created in late 1975. According to Dennis LeBlanc, "It was a natural pond that Ray Cornelius, the previous owner, had expanded, but it evaporated every summer. We brought in a bulldozer to dig it deeper. We then lined it with vinyl and covered the liner with dirt. From then on it was a year-around lake, in winter twelve to thirteen feet deep. During the summer, evaporation would take it down to seven or eight feet, but the vinyl lining prevented absorption into the soil." Reagan considered the building of the dock they built from the shore out into the lake one of his greatest accomplishments on the ranch.

From time to time Reagan waded into Lake Lucky to catch water snakes, dropping them in a sack and redepositing them in a willing neighbor's pond. As he extracted water snakes, he added goldfish. After several dozen died, he deduced they needed more oxygen, so he built an aerator system for them.

"Once the house was completed," says LeBlanc, " Governor Reagan always had his dining room chair face Lake Lucky; he really liked looking out at it at dinner time." In 1977, to commemorate their twenty-fifth wedding anniversary, Ronald Reagan gave his wife "Tru Luv," a canoe for Lake Lucky. He repeated his original proposal of marriage to her as they floated about the lake.

WORK OF ANOTHER SORT

Although the ranch occupied his thoughts and most of his spare time in those days, former Governor Reagan was increasingly urged by supporters around the country to seek the 1976 Republican presidential nomination. Wherever he landed for a speaking engagement, local volunteers would provide transportation and typically, their comments would be along the lines of, "You've been my candidate ever since you gave that famous speech for Goldwater in 1964," or "I heard your radio program today, and I agree with you completely."

One aspect of the agreement Mike Deaver and I had with Governor Reagan was that one of us would always accompany him on his speaking tours, which was usually seven to ten days a month. We heard these frequent expressions of support and received requests at every stop for meetings to talk with him about running for president.

While the political future occupied his mind much of the time, so did the ranch. I recall one flight home to California with him that summer. I looked over to find him gazing out the window, his thoughts far from the notes in his lap. "You have that ranch look in your eye," I said. "Yep, I sure do," he replied.

Even when "the ranch look" in his eye translated into work days at the ranch, he used the trips to and from his mountain retreat to write.

As Barney Barnett drove Nancy Reagan's red Ford station wagon, Governor Reagan would work on his speeches, radio scripts, and newspaper columns.

THE 1976 PRESIDENTIAL NOMINATION CAMPAIGN

One of those trips down the coast played a major role at the Republican National Convention in 1976.

Vice President Gerald Ford had succeeded Richard Nixon in August 1974, following Nixon's resignation. At one point, Ford said he would not run for a full term in 1976. Events changed his mind; but still pressure grew for a challenge. Despite calls to Reagan from many supporters to take up the challenge in 1975, for most of that year, he remained undecided, feeling that Ford should have the chance to succeed. By November, however, he decided to run, believing that the campaign process would pull the party closer to its conservative roots.

After initial losses in the 1976 primary elections to Ford, Reagan made a dramatic comeback in North Carolina in March. From then on, the campaign for delegates seesawed back and forth until, just before the party's convention in Kansas City in August, the count was virtually tied. On the second night of the convention, Tuesday the 17th, the Reagan organization, in order to pull the delegates it needed into its camp, mounted a rules fight intended to cement the delegates' loyalty. Our side narrowly lost that vote. Many delegates did not realize it, but the rules vote was a proxy for the presidential nomination balloting to take place the next night, Wednesday.

Wednesday morning, the Reagan senior staff assembled in his suite as he was finishing breakfast. Some supporters had called, urging him to take the vice presidency as Ford's running mate, Senator Richard Schweicker, Reagan's own choice for vice president, had offered to step aside if that would help Reagan's own presidential candidacy. Reagan said no, they came there together and they would leave together. What was not said was that all of us realized there would be no presidential candidacy. The nomination had been decided the night before.

After the meeting, a couple of us hung back. I said to Governor Reagan, "I guess we've never talked about an acceptance speech. Any idea of what you'd like to talk about in case the need arises?" He said that recently he had been asked to write a statement to go into a time capsule in Los Angeles, commemorating the city's bicentennial. He said the capsule was to be opened a century later. The story he then told us—of riding home after a recent ranch work day, looking out the car window at the Pacific Ocean and the Santa Ynez Mountains—became the basis for what turned out to be an unexpected speech the following night.

Thursday night was to feature President Ford's nomination acceptance speech. He gave a spirited and animated speech. Then he did an unprecedented thing; he invited Reagan, the defeated contestant, to the podium to speak. Some of us on Reagan's staff had learned just beforehand that Ford would do this; however, Governor Reagan himself did not know of it until Ford's public invitation. The Reagans left their box and proceeded to the stage.

Reagan's speech was a short one, but it had most eyes moist before it was over. He told the story of the time capsule. He said, "Suddenly it dawned on me. Those who read the letter [in the capsule] a hundred years from now will know whether those missiles were fired [he had posed the question of whether our defenses would be used in a future war]. They will know whether we met our challenge. Whether we will have the freedom that we have known up till now will depend on what we do here. Will they look back with appreciation and say, 'Thank God for those people in 1976 who headed off the loss of freedom; who kept us now, a hundred years later, free; who kept our world from nuclear destruction'?

"And, if we fail, they probably won't get to read the letter all because it spoke of individual freedom and they won't be allowed to talk of that or read of it. This is our challenge, and this is why we're here in this hall tonight." He ended with a stirring call for unity.

BACK TO WORK—AND THE RANCH

After Kansas City, there was time for vacation—that is, more days working in the sunshine of Rancho del Cielo—then a busy fall schedule. This meant that much of September and October were taken up with speaking tours, campaigning for the Ford-Dole ticket and many Congressional and state office candidates. Meanwhile, in September the five-day-a-week radio commentaries began again and the newspaper column had gone from once a week to twice a week. All this meant more writing on airplanes and in the station wagon on the way to and from the ranch.

According to Dennis LeBlanc, once most of the work at the ranch house was completed, by early 1977, their emphasis shifted to building fences, clearing brush from riding and hiking trails, and cutting and chopping wood for the two fireplaces which were the ranch house's only source of heat.

LeBlanc and Barney Barnett continued as Ronald Reagan's work partners. "He never asked Barney or me to do anything he wouldn't do," Dennis says. "It was wonderful to watch the two of them together. They were only a year apart in age, and their birthdays were on the same day, February 6. Barney would talk to him as if they were brothers. They'd be working on something and Barney would say, 'Damn it, Governor, you can't do it that way.' He'd reply, 'But Barney, I'm doing it.'

"He attributed his physical well-being, his longevity to being able to go to the ranch, both for the physical nature of the work and for riding his horses. He liked that adage, 'The best thing for the inside of a man is the outside of a horse.' He rode on an English saddle and everyone else up there rode Western. When you look at pictures of the group, he is always sitting straight as an arrow, while the others are slouching."

5
WELCOME TO RANCHO DEL CIELO

Although the Reagans did not refer to Rancho del Cielo as "The Western White House," they did enter into the spirit of the idea by naming the main road into the ranch "Pennsylvania Avenue."

You wind down Pennsylvania Avenue, emerging from a grove of oak trees to see the ranch house, its guest house, and guest-room trailer just below you. Next to it, an expanse of lawn leads to Lake Lucky and a tree-covered hill beyond. To the right is a large open pasture with a mountain rising beyond it, covered with trees on its lower slopes, then chaparral, and other native shrubs above. To the left, the road rises on a hill to reach the tack barn, about one hundred feet above the houses. Beyond it is the ranch foreman's cottage. To the left and further up the hill is the building that once housed the Secret Service command center. Beyond it is the hay barn and stable.

Pull up to the ranch house and you step out upon the covered sandstone entry patio laid by President Reagan. In front of you is the table and four pigskin-covered chairs which figured in photos of Reagan signing the historic 1981 tax bill, recording his Saturday radio broadcasts. It is also where the Reagans welcomed famous guests. The table and chairs are made in the Mexican equipal style—of bark tethered with bark.

THE RANCH HOUSE

Open the front door and you are in the L-shaped living room-dining room. You are immediately struck by the warm informality of the place. It is as if there had been a note on the front door: "We've gone for a ride; be back soon. Come in and make yourself comfortable—the Reagans."

To the left, inside the door, is a rock planter bed. Just to the right of the door is a hat rack, where President Reagan's sweat-stained dark blue baseball-type cap with the seal of the United States Mounted Secret Service above its bill hangs. This is the cap he often wore when he was clearing brush and cutting firewood. Opposite the cap is a Stetson. The hat rack is also home to a purse made from an armadillo shell, an Indian canteen covered in rawhide, an Irish *shillelagh,* and a leather firewood-carrier bag.

On the whitewashed walls hang Indian rugs. The polished red tile floors have scatter rugs, mostly Indian. The two halves of the "L" are about ten-by-fifteen feet each. On the outer wall of the living room half is a stone fireplace, flanked by two upholstered chairs. On the opposite wall are recessed bookshelves to the ceiling. An inset in the center holds Kenneth Wyatt's oil painting, "The Lame Horse," with a cowboy leading his horse back home in a downpour.

The bookshelves contain perhaps two hundred volumes covering a range of topics, but with the emphasis on California, the American West, and the outdoor life. Winston Churchill's *A History of the English-*

Speaking Peoples stands between *The Book of the American West* and Larry McMurtry's *Lonesome Dove.* Nearby are *Spanish Colonial or Adobe Architecture of California, 1800-1850; The Indian and the Horse;* and Theodore Roosevelt's *African Game Trails.*

Below the bookshelves are rattan armchairs and a settee with a reading light on a table between them.

From waist height upward, the outer walls of the dining room half of the L-shaped room are all glass, with a view of Lake Lucky, the green lawn and the trees and mountain beyond. There are six chairs at the table. The president always sat at the end of the table facing the view.

As you face the dining room, just to the left of the dining table, below the windows is an oak loveseat rocker with a rattan seat. A single rocker faces it, on the other side of a bumper-pool table. In that section of the room there is a pass-through to the bar-kitchen. At the end of the room is a door leading to the maid's room and bath.

Opposite the bar hangs a mounted pair of "jackalopes." A "jackalope" is actually concocted from a jackrabbit head and a pair of antlers. A set of green Mexican goblets stands on a rack, as if the president himself might come around the corner to offer you a drink; his own preference, when he drank at all, was a single vodka-and-orange juice.

The small, but efficient kitchen is all electric. A rack of spices sits on the counter, as if ready to be used for dinner. Salt and pepper shakers, cream pitcher, and sugar bowl are also at the ready. The kitchen window looks out toward the guest house.

A door between the bar and kitchen leads into the high-ceilinged den, which was the main room of the original adobe cottage. Like the living room, which it adjoins, its dominant colors are soft reds, oranges, yellows, and browns. It has a polished tile floor, which is covered with cowhide and sheepskin rugs. This is where the Reagans spent much of their leisure time. There is a large stone fireplace in one corner. Along with the living room fireplace, it is the house's only source of heat. There are two comfortable sofas at a right angle to one another under the room's one window. Over one hangs Robert Rishell's painting, "The Golden State," a gift from Reagan's gubernatorial staff when he left Sacramento. It depicts soft, late afternoon sunshine on a typical coastal California scene of oaks and golden hills. Although it wasn't painted at Rancho del Cielo, it looks as if it could have been.

In one corner is a large armoire hiding a Zenith television set. There are three armchairs grouped about, one with a hassock.

Just beyond the den is the master bedroom, done primarily in soft yellow. On the bed is a patchwork quilt, yellow and blue made in the Around-the-World style by a Vermont quilter who sent it to the Reagans as a gift. Sheepskin rugs are on either side of the bed. Rotary telephones sit on one nightstand.

The room also has a small table and two cowhide-covered chairs, a reprise of the Mexican equipal table-and-chairs set on the front patio. While the outdoor set is in natural bark and hide colors, the bedroom set is yellow.

The Reagans' clothes hang in the closet. On one side are his Stetsons, riding boots, a White House jacket, one of his favorite polo shirts for horseback riding, and his riding breeches; on the other, Nancy Reagan's ranch and riding wear.

The Guest House

Like the main house, the two-bedroom guest house is comfortably, but simply furnished. Western prints hang on its walls and a small bookcase holds a selection of books from the main house. The trailer beyond it, which looks like a small building, was dubbed "The Ranchhand Trailer." It has a single bed at either end, and served as quarters for Dennis LeBlanc and Barney Barnett when they accompanied the Reagans on ranch work sessions.

The Tack Barn

Some fifty steps above the lawn outside the ranch house is the metal building that contains the well-equipped tack room as well as a garage for the two presidential Jeeps. One, a blue 1982 model, with front and back seats and a cargo bed, was a gift to Reagan from long-time friends. It has two license plates: California's "4 RR" with a 1984 Olympics logo, and another, from the 1985 Presidential Inaugural, that reads "Gipper." This Jeep replaced a 1962 red model, still on hand.

According to John Barletta, who for several years was in charge of Reagan's Secret Service detail, Reagan loved driving the Jeep during his presidency. "As president he wasn't allowed to drive except here. He would use the Jeep to go out to clear brush and cut wood."

Next to the Jeeps is a drive-yourself lawn mower with the presidential seal above its front grill. Nearby is a well-equipped work bench and tool racks.

A Rancho del Cielo Album

1. Pure relaxation!

2. In front of the ranch house, February, 1985.

3. *By Lake Lucky, August, 1983.*

4. *First Lady and friend, June, 1983.*

5. *The Reagans in "Tru Luv" on Lake Lucky, August, 1983.*

6. Rancho del Cielo before it was Rancho del Cielo, c. 1935.

7. Ranch house, guest houses, Secret Service command post on hill, April, 1983.

8. Looking out to the Santa Ynez valley from the ranch.

9. Ranch house, guest house and trailer guest room, April, 1983.

10. The ranch house from the shore of Lake Lucky (facing the dining room area).

11. Sign at the entrance to the big pasture.

12. The address sign that hangs over the front entry.

13. A rare snowfall brings down a tree (inspected by Courtney Trisler, Rancho del Cielo foreman, 1985 to 2001).

14. *The grave of "No Strings," Mrs. Reagan's favorite horse, in the animal cemetery at Rancho del Cielo, also known as "Boot Hill."*

15. *Heart Rock.*

16. The ranch house living room.

17. Another view of the living room.

18. The ranch house living room looking toward the dining room.

19. The den, looking toward the front door.

20. Patio at the front of the house.

21. By the front door.

22. The ranch house dining room.

23. Recreation area corner of the L-shaped living/dining room.

24. The ranch
house bar.

25. The
guest house
living room.

26. *Chain of Title certificate.*

27. *A Reagan favorite: jelly beans.*

28. *The presidential closet.*

29. The "jackalopes."

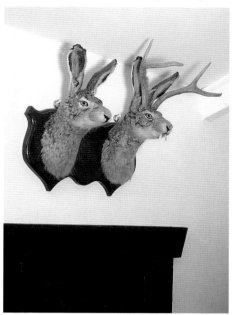

30. The railroad bell by the tack barn.

31. The tack room.

32. *Time for the morning ride.*

33. Riding the stallion El Alamein, a gift from President Lopez Portillo of Mexico.

34. Grooming El Alamein, c. 1982.

35. The Reagans on the trail.

36, 37. Some of the Reagans' four-footed friends.

38. *The Reagans on the trail with John Barletta of the Secret Service following, February, 1985.*

39. Relaxing outside the tack barn after the morning ride, July, 1982.

40. *Working with the chainsaw.*

41. A wood chopping day from the late 1970s.

42. He cut every log himself! August, 1988.

43. Ronald Reagan at the wheel, August, 1985.

44. On a fence wire hauling mission by Jeep, April, 1984.

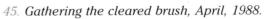
45. Gathering the cleared brush, April, 1988.

*46. Taking
a break from
chopping wood.*

47. Meeting with then Vice-President George H. W. Bush, August, 1985.

*48. Signing
the tax bill,
August, 1981.*

49. Greeting Queen Elizabeth II (and Prince Philip) in the rain, February, 1983.

50. A serenade at Nancy Reagan's birthday party (William Wilson next to President Reagan), August, 1987.

51. The daily national security briefing (President Reagan, with Chief of Staff Howard Baker and National Security Advisor Colin Powell), August, 1987.

52. The hat rack just inside the front door.

The wood-paneled tack room looks as if it is ready for "The Gipper" to step right in to pick up saddles and bridles to get ready for a ride. A collection of oiled-and-polished saddles flanks the two walls, each with its pad and girth. Bridles and reins hang on their hooks. The walls are covered with pictures of the Reagans and their horses.

The former Secret Service command center is in a plain metal building, unobtrusively tucked behind a stand of oak trees on the hillside above the tack barn. At present it is unused. The Young America's Foundation, which purchased the ranch in April 1998, is considering using the former command center building as a reception center for the students it brings up to the ranch for tours and talks about the fortieth president and his record.

THE PET CEMETERY

Imagine we are walking back to the main house where we meet the ranch foreman who takes us in his four-wheel-drive pickup truck around through the big pasture to the hill on the opposite side. There, in the sunlight, filtered between oak trees and several unusually large and imposing red-bark madrone trees, is the pet cemetery, sometimes called Boot Hill. Reagan thought of the ranch animals as part of his family. Here are the graves of beloved dogs, horses, a bull, and a cow.

The first lady's favorite horse, No Strings, was buried here in 1992. The president's favorite mount, Little Man, is there, too. Kelly, a horse from the Royal Canadian Mounted Police, was buried in 1990. Duke and Duchess, the bull and cow, died in 1999. There are several dogs, including Rhino, the ranch's first. Nearby are Fuzzy, Rex, Millie, Taca, Lucky, Kodiak, Frebo, Victory, and the late Maureen Reagan's small poodle, Barnae (originally meant to have been named in honor of Barney Barnett until it was discovered "he" was a "she").

Ronald Reagan carved nearly all of the sandstone headstones himself. When he spotted a likely stone, he would have it brought to the workshop where he would do the carving when the time came. The letters and dates were then painted and, in recent years, repainted by a Santa Barbara volunteer, Karl Mull.

* * *

Stand in the soft light of the pet cemetery and you can feel the warm, straightforward humanity of its creator.

6
SAFE AND SOUND

During his 1976 campaign for the Republican nomination for president, Ronald Reagan had Secret Service protection through the party's convention in mid-August that year. Throughout the campaign he was able to make occasional work visits to the ranch. As a candidate and not president, he had none of the elaborate communications and security installations that were made later at the ranch.

It was in 1976 that his Secret Service detail gave Ronald and Nancy Reagan the code names "Rawhide" and "Rainbow," respectively. The names stuck from then on and seemed especially apt in the ranch setting, with the president's love of the outdoors and the bright, cheerful home the First Lady had created.

By 1980, when he was the front-runner for the nomination and then, ultimately, the nominee, ranch visits were infrequent and brief. Martin Anderson, a senior aide at the time, recalls one of them. One day the campaign took Reagan and his entourage to the Santa Ynez Valley, just north of the mountains where the ranch is located.

There was some "down time" between two events and the campaign crew was resting at an inn. According to Anderson, Reagan said, "We're not far from the ranch. I wonder how long it would take to get there?" He asked his Secret Service agents if there was time to go to the ranch before the next event. Anderson says, "They weren't keen about it, but up we went on Refugio Pass Road in two or three cars. When we got there, Reagan got out and walked over to the fence, beyond which was the big pasture. Suddenly, we heard the sound of galloping hooves and it was his horses coming right to him. He patted their necks and talked to them. We couldn't have been there more than thirty minutes, but it was important to him just to see the place and touch those horses."

Rather than being impromptu visitors, the Secret Service became a permanent presence at Rancho del Cielo after Reagan's election as president on November 4 that year. According to the Secret Service's John Barletta who had been assigned to President Jimmy Carter since 1978, "I first saw the ranch after the November 1980 election, during the transition. When a new president comes in the Secret Service divides the existing presidential detail. Half goes to the incoming president and half stays with the outgoing president, supplemented by other agents to make up the difference. Even though Reagan had Secret Service protection while he was running for office, it's different after the election. For example, we had to become acquainted with all the locations he might visit regularly—such as the ranch."

The Secret Service created a new unit at the time, the Western Protective Division. According to Barletta, this division was responsible for protecting the ranch even when he wasn't there. The Service developed its own detailed topographic map of the property and created an electronic protection system around its perimeter. A helicopter pad was created, and sophisticated communications equipment installed so the president could be in constant contact with Washington on secure telephone and fax lines. Working and overnight quarters for on-duty agents were screened by trees and shrubs to make them as unobtrusive as possible.

The Disney Corporation produced several imitation boulders to house motion detectors and other electronic sensors. Numbers were emblazoned on rocks along the riding trails to help track the presidential party when it was on horseback.

Work began on the command center building in late 1980, during the presidential transition. While it was being built, the Secret Service detail used recreational vehicles as temporary offices. "Our shifts changed three times a day," John Barletta recalls. "That meant a lot of commuting [from Santa Barbara, where the agents were housed] and the vehicles took a beating. You'd go through a set of brakes and tires every 10,000 miles, but we never had an accident. In addition to the main road, we also improved the dirt road up the backside of the ranch from Santa Ynez Valley so that it would be available in case of emergency. It's no longer usable."

Throughout his eight presidential years, Reagan arrived and departed by helicopter, with a single exception when bad weather kept the helicopter grounded.

There was only one vehicle accident on the ranch during those years, according to Barletta. One time, when Barney Barnett was driving the Jeep, it slipped down an embankment on to its side. "Barney had some cuts, scratches, and a dislocated elbow," Barletta says. "He was crawling up the embankment toward us when we found him. An agent called the command post to get medical attention. He neglected to say that the president wasn't involved. They sent the helicopter up to the ranch, thinking he was. Instead, President Reagan was helping clean up Barney, and I put Barney's elbow in a sling. He went to the hospital. The news media people were all waiting, expecting to have a story about the president!"

Barletta accompanied President Reagan or preceded him on every one of the president's visits to the ranch during the White House years. "Like all the other agents," he says, "I've traveled all over the world, but when I first saw Santa Barbara, never in my wildest dreams did I think I'd be living here, let alone retiring here." Yet, in 1987, the Secret Service transferred him permanently to Santa Barbara as the agent in charge of ranch security for the remainder of Reagan's term. In 1989, Barletta became Assistant Special Agent in Charge of the Secret Service detail assigned to President Reagan after he left office, and in 1997 Barletta retired to Santa Barbara.

The Mounted Secret Service

Other than the constant monitoring of security and communications systems, a typical ranch day for the Secret Service would begin at 6 a.m., when the morning shift relieved the night shift. Barletta would check in then. Shortly after, along with the three other agents who would also ride, he got his horse ready. They would bring the horses down from the stable to the tack barn. President Reagan would come up from the house "and we'd go over the map to decide where he wanted to ride," Barletta says. "He'd always ask if that was where 'the fellows' would like to ride. He always wanted us to have a good ride, too. Then he'd point out a route he thought we'd all enjoy and I'd call the command post to tell them which sector of the ranch we'd be in.

"The president would get Mrs. Reagan's horse ready, then he'd ring the bell—Mrs. Reagan's grandfather's railroad bell—which was mounted on a post opposite the barn. Then we were off, usually for a couple of hours at least."

On rainy days, according to Barletta, "The president would say, 'Well, we can't ride,' so we'd go into the tack room and he'd start telling stories. Barney would say, 'Governor, remember the time....' and start a new story. I'd sit there, fascinated. A new agent asked me why Barney always called him 'Governor.' I replied, 'He's the only one who got away with that.' It was a term of endearment and respect."

INTRUDERS

There were a few instances of people prowling about during the Western White House years, but usually when the president was not there. "We'd patrol and catch an occasional hiker or biker," Barletta notes. "We'd check them for weapons, but most of them didn't even realize they were on private property—despite the signs. We did receive occasional intelligence communiqués that something was going to happen, but it never did."

Reagan, in his memoirs, recounts the Secret Service's encounter with a four-legged intruder: "One day an agent came down from his post on the hill above the house, and his eyes were wide as saucers.

He'd been sitting on his camp stool watching the house when a big mountain lion . . . strolled past him only a few feet away. . . ."

7
WESTERN WHITE HOUSE DAYS

From time to time, every U.S. president has longed to get away from the pressures of the job. Living under the public spotlight day-in and day-out increases the attractiveness of the distant family home or farm or special retreat where nature is close at hand.

The public spotlight's beam focuses on the president all of his time in office, plus for a few years on the way there, but for Ronald Reagan virtually his entire career was a public one. His first job was at WOC, a radio station in Davenport, Iowa. Hired in the fall of 1932, he was, at first, an obscure and anonymous radio announcer. This soon changed, and by the time he moved to its sister station, WHO, Des Moines, he was recreating Chicago Cubs baseball games and gaining a personal following.

Among other things, he joined the Army's Cavalry reserve and learned to ride horseback, in time becoming a skilled rider. Later, in Western movies, rather than using stand-ins, he rode in all his equestrian scenes.

In the spring of 1937, he accompanied the Cubs to Santa Catalina Island, off the Southern California coast, to cover spring training. One outcome of the trip was a Warner Brothers screen test and a contract offer. His film career was launched. Over the next twenty-five years, he appeared in more than fifty feature-length films.

By the 1950s, the focus of his career changed, but he was still very much in the public eye as host of television's "The General Electric Hour," a weekly drama broadcast live, in which he occasionally starred as well.

In the late 1940s, as president of the Screen Actors Guild, he was in another sort of public spotlight, testifying before Congress about the efforts of Communists to take over some Hollywood unions.

Reagan's General Electric contract called for him to make periodic visits to GE plants around the country. There he would meet workers coming off shifts, make brief remarks, then open the floor to questions and comments. This proved to be the forerunner of his favorite form of campaigning in later years. Following his GE years, he was host of television's "Death Valley Days."

In 1964, shortly before the presidential election, he gave a nationally broadcast television address in support of Barry Goldwater's candidacy. It raised an unprecedented amount of money in contributions. After Goldwater's defeat, many conservatives who had seen "the speech"—as it came to be called—saw in Reagan a new leader for the conservative movement.

Elective office became a reality with Reagan's landslide victory over incumbent California Governor Edmund G. "Pat" Brown in 1966. From then until his retirement from the White House in January 1989, Ronald Reagan was constantly a public figure.

For one whose life had been largely in the public eye for decades, Rancho del Cielo represented a special haven of privacy. Two weeks at the ranch during a presidential year became the equivalent of those periods between film assignments in earlier years when he could relax totally and enjoy his family.

Ronald and Nancy Reagan's marriage has been an especially close one. Indeed, it is probably one of America's great love stories of modern times. Time at the ranch meant time for them to be away from public duties, together, in a setting all their own.

Edwin Meese III, a senior official in both the Reagan governor's office and the White House and later U.S. Attorney General, put it this way: "He would work hard, both at his official duties and at the ranch. He liked the time there to recharge his batteries, to be by himself and with Nancy. The ranch reflects his love of the outdoors and the importance to him of getting away from the machinations of politics. The wide open spaces—blue sky and clear air—really appealed to him." After President Reagan took office, the Reagans sold their long-time home in the Pacific Palisades section of Los Angeles. The ranch then became their legal and voting residence.

The Reagans did little large-scale entertaining at the ranch. The closest thing was Nancy Reagan's annual birthday party on July 7. Their circle of close social friends had made this a tradition over several years and it continued during the Western White House years. Betty Wilson and Marion Jorgenson, as they had for some time, orchestrated the events.

The two women and their husbands, William Wilson and Earle Jorgenson, were occasional weekend visitors at the ranch and would join the Reagans on their horseback rides.

Paul Laxalt* remembers a time when he and a group from the Rancheros Visitadores stopped by Rancho del Cielo. Each summer the group observed a tradition begun in Spanish colonial days, when groups of central coast ranchers would spend a week or so on horseback, visiting neighboring ranches, and enjoying the hospitality of their hosts.

FAMOUS GUESTS

A number of famous guests visited during the presidential years. Queen Elizabeth II and Prince Philip arrived for lunch in a torrential rainstorm on February 1, 1983.

President Reagan had ridden in Windsor Park with the queen the year before, but there was no possibility of returning the favor at Rancho del Cielo. The Secret Service's John Barletta recalls, "It was raining so hard I thought the horses would sink to their knees in the mud if we were to try to go riding." At the time, the president apologized for the bad weather. "Don't apologize," the queen replied, "It makes me feel right at home."

The royal couple returned to their yacht, *Britannia,* anchored off Santa Barbara. They took Mrs. Reagan with them on the voyage north to San Francisco. There the president joined them for a shipboard

* Paul Laxalt and Ronald Reagan became friends when they were governors of neighboring states. Laxalt went on to represent Nevada in the United States Senate from December 18, 1974-January 3, 1987. After serving two terms-plus, he did not stand for reelection in 1986. He was chairman of Reagan's 1976 and 1980 presidential campaigns and General Chairman of the Republican National Committee during Reagan's presidency.

celebration in honor of the Reagans' forthcoming wedding anniversary. At the dinner, Nancy Reagan said, "What more could a girl ask?" Ronnie rose and said, "I know I promised Nancy a lot of things thirty-one years ago, but I never promised her *this.*"

On August 1, 1984, Presidential Press Secretary Larry Speakes escorted Papal Nuncio Archbishop Pio Laghi from Santa Barbara to the ranch by helicopter. There, the Vatican's envoy to the U.S. conferred with the president over a working lunch about the U.S. response to a Polish parliamentary decree that called for the release of Polish political prisoners. National Security Adviser Robert McFarlane joined them in the discussion. This event reflected the close cooperation between the administration and the Vatican to advance the Reagan Doctrine* and help democratic movements behind the "Iron Curtain."

In August 1985, George and Barbara Bush spent an afternoon at the ranch. President Reagan and then-Vice President Bush discussed international trade issues.

On February 5, 1991, not long after she had left office as British Prime Minister, Margaret Thatcher joined the Reagans for a day at the ranch where she and the former president discussed the shape of the post-Cold War world.

Mikhail Gorbachev, no longer in office, and his wife, Raisa, called on the Reagans on May 3, 1992. Reagan took Gorbachev for a tour of the property in his blue Jeep with both an American and a Russian secret service agent in the back seat.

* The Reagan Doctrine, in essence, was the commitment to aid democratic movements in Communist-dominated countries, through all non-military means, until they became free.

Washington Post correspondent Lou Cannon relates that the pair posed for news cameras wearing Stetson hats. Reagan had just given one to Gorbachev, who reciprocated with the gift of a book of Russian proverbs. "Gorby said that this photo would be even more famous than the ones taken at their Geneva summit in 1985. In the photos you can see Reagan looking at Gorbachev's hat, which is on backwards, but Reagan is too polite to say anything. I heard afterward that Reagan mentioned it to him. I don't know if something got lost in the translation, but Gorbachev continued to wear it backwards."

Because by then the Soviet Union was no more, it is said that much of their conversation centered on horses, home improvement, and real estate prices.

At the time, Gorbachev was on a cross-country tour that included visits to then-President George Bush and former President Jimmy Carter; however, the Reagan visit was first on his presidential itinerary. The day after his ranch visit, Gorbachev received an award at the Ronald Reagan Presidential Library.

Canadian Premier Brian Mulroney and his wife, Mila, visited the Reagans at the ranch for a day in April 1993, just two months before Mulroney, himself, retired from public life.

THE MORNING RIDE

Early mornings at the Western White House, President Reagan devoted to what he called his "Washington homework." Then, about 9, he rang the bell outside the tack barn to summon the First Lady for their daily ride. John Barletta would ride abreast of the president. Mrs. Reagan and another agent rode right behind them. Further in the distance, and not seen in the many photos taken by the White House photographers of them on their rides, was a Hummer. This custom all-terrain adaptation of the squat, wide-tread military vehicle, held several more Secret Service agents, their weapons, medical emergency equipment, telephones, and the "football," the case containing the nation's nuclear-missile launch codes, which needed always to be close to the president wherever he was.

Riding was more casual in pre-presidential days. Martin Anderson recalls Reagan telling him that in earlier days he would sometimes ride out on the back trails with a .38-caliber pistol armed with shot shell. "I'd use it to shoot rattlesnakes from the saddle," he told Anderson.

The presidential rides would often take them to a favored high point where, as Reagan once put it, "You can watch boats cruising across the Santa Barbara Channel, then turn your head and see the Santa Ynez Valley unfold like a huge wilderness amphitheater before your eyes."

Heart Rock was another trail ride landmark. This large sandstone block, at the intersection of two trails, carried the initials "RR + NR" within a heart, carved by Reagan himself in August 1977. Later, other family members added their own initials.

Bright sunlight gave way to dappled light as they rode through oak and madrone clusters. Suddenly, the view would be of large open spaces and full sunlight again.

At the end of each ride, back at the tack barn, the president would dismount first, help the First Lady off her horse, then give her a hug and a kiss.

The President had summoned the First Lady to the ride by ringing a bell at the tack barn. At lunch time, the process was reversed, when she rang a bell outside the ranch house kitchen to summon him to the midday meal.

Unless there was more "Washington homework," Reagan devoted his afternoons to clearing brush, chopping wood, and other ranch chores.

WORLD AFFAIRS

Before the ride, President Reagan's day at the Western White House would begin with presidential business. First was the daily national security briefing. As often as not, this was done by a secure telephone line, with the national security adviser who was in Santa Barbara. According to Richard Allen, Reagan's first national security adviser, "Some days we would send it in written form by courier." Some times it was done in person.

Nancy Reagan recalled, "[You] could forget the world for a few hours, but every day a government car would drive up the mountain with a big envelope of mail, security documents, and newspapers."

William Clark, Reagan's second national security adviser (who also had been an early chief of staff in the governor's office, then a member of the state Supreme Court, then U.S. Deputy Secretary of State), recalls, "We felt if we could do it by secure phone or courier, we would." When in-person briefings were needed, according to Clark, "I'd sometimes take an expert [on the particular subject] along. He could brief the president directly instead of my 'translating' for him."

The Reagans were at the ranch when a Soviet missile shot down a Korean airliner, flight KAL 007, on September 8, 1983. Clark recalled, "Bill Casey [Director of Central Intelligence] called me and I flashed it to the president immediately. It was then late afternoon in California. The report was that the Soviets had possibly shot down an unarmed commercial airliner. I had been just about to join John Poindexter for dinner. The president's reaction was typical of him. 'Well, Bill, let's pray that it didn't happen. If it's confirmed that it did occur, with all that we have going on with arms negotiations, let's not overreact.' He said John and I should go on to dinner and not sit around waiting for the phone to ring. Once the tragedy was confirmed, he decided to cut his ranch stay short and return to Washington."

Clark recalls another time, in September 1981, when, as deputy secretary of state, he saw Egyptian President Anwar Sadat off on his trip home from Washington. "We had just sold fighter planes to Israel and they were about to be delivered. Sadat told me he didn't know how he would explain that to his people. I said I would take it up with Secretary of State Alexander Haig. I did and we decided to call the president. He came in from chopping wood to take the call. He said, 'Delay the delivery and let that wonderful man return home in peace.' The delay did occur, but Sadat was assassinated when he returned home."

Clark sums up the function of the Western White House this way: "When he was there as president, the ranch was a critical place from which decisions were made—perhaps not with the same frequency as in the Oval Office, but he was always on call. The continuity of the presidency was never broken; nor did he ever apologize for being there. We were satisfied that he was totally accessible and available. Usually, there was no reason to awaken him in the night, but we had standing orders from him that he be notified if we lost any armed services personnel overseas."

The Reagans were at the ranch in March 1986 when the president was notified that a terrorist's bomb had exploded in a Berlin disco, killing an American soldier and a Turkish woman, and injuring fifty U.S. servicemen and more than one hundred civilians. Evidence pointed directly to Muammar Qaddafi's Libyan government. This led to a retaliatory U.S. air attack on Qaddafi's military headquarters on April 14. Reagan, back at the Oval Office, addressed the nation:

> We tried quiet diplomacy, public condemnation, economic sanctions and demonstrations of military force. None succeeded. Despite our repeated warnings, Qaddafi continued his reckless policy of intimidation, his relentless pursuit of terror. He counted on America to be passive. He counted wrong. I warned that there should be no place on earth where terrorists can rest and train and practice their deadly skills. I meant it. I said that we would act with others, if possible, and alone if necessary, to insure that terrorists have no sanctuary anywhere. Tonight, we have.

On another occasion, in summer 1987, Secretary of State George Shultz returned home via the ranch to give Reagan a personal report on his meetings in Moscow with President Mikhail Gorbachev and Foreign Minister Eduard Shevardnadze. The subject was preparation for the Reagan-Gorbachev summit to be held in Washington that December. After conferring with the president, Shultz went to Santa Barbara to brief the White House press corps there.

Kenneth Duberstein, Reagan's last chief of staff, recalls a spring 1987 Reagan ranch sojourn when he, then deputy chief of staff, Chief of Staff Howard Baker, and other senior staff members held what amounted to a planning seminar in Santa Barbara to discuss strategy for the president's final year-and-a-half in office. They conferred with Reagan several times during the course of their discussions, mostly by conference telephone call, with Reagan at the ranch and the staff group at the Santa Barbara Biltmore Hotel.

Signing the Tax Bill

In his first year as president, 1981, Ronald Reagan worked with tenacity and single-mindedness to achieve his first major objective: passage of an across-the-board, growth-oriented tax cut bill. He achieved this with the passage in the Senate of what came to be known as The Economic Recovery Act. On August 13, a few days after its passage, he signed the bill at the ranch, at the patio table in front of the ranch house. A pool of about twenty reporters and cameras were on hand to record the event.

The bill ushered in the largest tax-cut program in the nation's history up to that time. In time, it had the effects Reagan had anticipated. It triggered a ninety-two-month period of economic growth, unbroken from November 1982 to July 1990. Reagan's popularity, coupled with his intense personal lobbying of members of Congress of both parties, played a major role in the passage of the bill, which remained one of his proudest achievements and which accounts for his broad smile as he signed the bill.

RADIO DAYS

One day between Ronald Reagan's election in November 1980 and his inauguration as the fortieth President of the United States the next January, Michael Deaver, who was to become White House deputy chief of staff, telephoned Harry O'Connor, the man who had produced and syndicated Reagan's popular five-day-a-week radio commentaries for nearly five years in 1975-79.

What, he asked, did O'Connor think of the idea of a weekly presidential radio commentary? O'Connor thought it was a good one. It would punctuate quiet weekends with a story for the Sunday newspapers. Even if not many stations actually broadcast the commentary, he reasoned, radio and television networks would use excerpts from it in their weekend news broadcasts.

Thus, Ronald Reagan established what is, in Harry O'Connor's words, "a fixture"—and which continues today, three presidents later. During his presidency, Reagan taped thirty-five of his weekly commentaries from the ranch, most from the patio table by the front door of the ranch house.

These were taped on Saturday mornings, usually between 9:06 and 9:11, for release to all stations and networks shortly thereafter.

THANKSGIVING

The Reagans spent every Thanksgiving during his presidency at the ranch. It was a family time. The 1983 holiday was typical. The White House press secretary's temporary Santa Barbara office released this notice on Thanksgiving Day, November 24:

> Shortly before arriving at Rancho del Cielo yesterday, the President surveyed the ranch property in a jeep. After the survey, he returned to the residence and had dinner with Mrs. Reagan.
>
> Because the weather at the Ranch is overcast, cold, and rainy, the President and Mrs. Reagan will not go horseback riding today. The President will spend the morning on routine paperwork.
>
> Maureen Reagan and her husband, Dennis Revell, are expected to arrive at the Ranch early this afternoon. Patti Davis and Neil Reagan and his wife, Bess, are expected to arrive at the Ranch at approximately 3:00 p.m. PST. The Reagan family will have Thanksgiving dinner at approximately 5:00 p.m. PST and the menu will be:

Turkey

Cornbread dressing

Giblet gravy

Peas

Mashed potatoes

Fresh cranberry mold

Monkey bread and jam

Olives

Carrots

Celery strips

Apple pie

Pumpkin pie

8
STOP THE PRESSES?

Reporters who are assigned to cover presidents when they are on retreat find that the experience involves long periods of inactivity when there is no news, punctuated by occasional excitement—and headlines.

This has long been true. In 1927, while President Calvin Coolidge and his family were relaxing in a camp in the Black Hills of South Dakota and while he indulged his hobby of fishing, the handful of reporters assigned to cover him sat about the simple press room arranged for them at a high school in Rapid City. There was little to report until one August day the president asked them to assemble, whereupon he handed each a slip of paper with the words, "I do not choose to run for President in Nineteen Twenty-eight." He took no questions and left. Coolidge biographer Claude M. Fuess writes, "there was a wild scramble for the nearest telegraph office and long-distance telephone."

A small sign on the front door of the main house at Rancho del Cielo may have proved prophetic for reporters covering President Reagan during his sojourns there. It reads:

On This Site in 1897

Nothing Happened

Here is a typical daily report from the Reagan staff during a summer Rancho del Cielo retreat:

THE WHITE HOUSE
Office of the Press Secretary
(Santa Barbara, California)

NOTICE TO THE PRESS
August 24, 1985

Following breakfast with Mrs. Reagan at the residence at Rancho del Cielo, the President delivered his weekly radio address. Following the radio address, the President was interviewed by representatives of three radio stations. The President will spend part of the morning on routine paperwork and is expected to go horseback riding. Following lunch with Mrs. Reagan, the President is expected to take a walk on the ranch property.

The weather at Rancho del Cielo is sunny and warm.

Despite the sybaritic climate and atmosphere of Santa Barbara, the reporters and camera crews assigned to cover Reagan's ranch visits were under pressure to file a daily story, and the sameness of his days left them frustrated.

THE DAILY "RANCH REPORT"

ABC's Sam Donaldson put it this way: "When he was up at the ranch, the hardest decision the reporters had to make was where to go for dinner. There was no real news, just the routine 'ranch report' every day. One night, I was talking live with Barbara Walters on 20/20 and she asked me what was going on. I said, 'Nothing much. We have the ranch report here and, once again, he chopped wood and cleared brush. I suspect that just before he gets there, they haul up truckloads of brush and wood for him to chop because, if he chopped as much as they say he does, there wouldn't be any trees left on the ranch.'

"Well, Reagan was watching, and the next day, I'm told, he called his ranch foreman and said he wanted all the brush he had cleared over the last week or ten days piled up in one place by the house. They did, and he had a photographer take pictures of it from all angles. He sent me one of the photos, on which he had written, 'Dear Sam: Here's proof I chopped it all with my own little hatchet.' Talk about focus!"

Despite the dearth of news in a normal Rancho del Cielo day, there was always the possibility that something big would break—and occasionally it did. Thus, major news organizations regularly stationed crews in Santa Barbara and had access to the presidential press secretary and other senior staff members, also stationed in the city.

Regulars were the *Washington Post, Washington Times, Baltimore Sun, New York Times,* New York *Daily News, Chicago Tribune, Los Angeles Times, The Wall Street Journal,* and *USA Today.* The major news magazines, *Time, Newsweek,* and *U.S. News & World Report* were there, as were the wire services, Associated Press, United Press International, Reuter, and Agence France-Presse. Network television crews from ABC, CBS, NBC, and CNN were always on hand.

Newspaper chains such as Knight-Ridder were often represented, and the local newspaper, the *Santa Barbara News-Press,* was always on the lookout for any Reagan ranch news. According to the *Washington Post's* Lou Cannon, who covered most of Reagan's political career in both Sacramento and Washington and is the author of several well-regarded books about Reagan, the usual contingent was fifty to sixty media people, "This might swell to one hundred depending upon the occasion."

"Santa Barbara duty" was much sought-after by many reporters. John McCaslin, now a *Washington Times* columnist, was a young reporter covering the Reagan White House in 1984-85, junior to the late Jeremiah O'Leary. He says, "Jerry allowed me my choice of trips with Reagan, each journey being historically memorable, but when it came time for Reagan to visit his ranch, Jerry drew the line. I can still hear him say, 'The world's most beautiful spot this side of County Kerry, Ireland, is the view from my hotel room overlooking the Santa Barbara beach'."

The press center was at the Santa Barbara Sheraton Hotel, at the south end of Cabrillo Boulevard, which went the length of the beach. Originally the Mar Monte Hotel, popular with wintering Midwesterners when it was built in the 1920s, and today the Radisson, the hotel was the site of daily briefings by the presidential press secretary, and most of the working press stayed there. CBS Television's producer, Susan Zirinsky, said her network arranged to always have the same rooms and laid their own telephone lines into those rooms under the beds.

A few writers who did not feel the need for daily briefings moved to the Santa Barbara Biltmore (now the Four Seasons Biltmore). One reason cited by Cannon is that "the more important Reagan staff members were at the Biltmore. One of the cottages there had the National Security staff's equipment. If you needed to see the National Security Adviser, say, rather than the press secretary, that was the place to be."

REPORTING ON-SITE

When President Reagan taped his Saturday radio broadcasts from the ranch, a press pool was assigned to be there, recording the event even though the White House communications team made the official feed. Other than that there were few times when the news media were invited to cover the president on-site.

This was a contrast to Jimmy Carter's retreats at his home in Plains, Georgia. About Carter, Susan Zirinsky of CBS recalls, "We staked him out every day as he went about Plains. We followed him—about three feet behind—and he would talk with us as we went along. Each of the three broadcast networks had a mobile home rigged up as a studio/office under the town water tower. This little trailer park was just five blocks from the Carter's home. Santa Barbara, by contrast, was a lot more beautiful, but access to Reagan was severely limited because he was twenty-seven miles away on a mountaintop."

Reagan's signing of the Economy Recovery Act of 1981—the big across-the-board tax-cut bill—on August 13 that year was a major news occasion. A pool of reporters and camera crews went up to the ranch for the event, which took place in the fog on the front patio. "I think the tax bill signing was the most exciting thing I covered at the ranch," Lou Cannon recalls. The most memorable was one that occurred when I wasn't there. I had taken a few days off from 'ranch duty.' That was when the Korean airliner was shot down by the Soviets in 1983. Reagan wanted to stay at the ranch, saying that they could handle the issue from there. You could, but it was pretty awful public relations. I never had the feeling that people cared whether he took two weeks or five days there, but there was a feeling that, in a crisis, he ought to be back at the center, the White House.

"At the time of the KAL incident," according to Cannon, "the Reagan people were getting that reaction—[Deputy Chief of Staff] Mike Deaver and [National Security Adviser] Bill Clark, for example." CBS's Susan Zirinsky notes, "When the KAL story broke our camera showed him doing the usual things around the ranch. He was taking care of business, of course, but visually the impression was that he was disengaged."

Reagan delayed for a day, then went back to Washington. It was only a day or two prior to his originally scheduled departure for the capital, according to Bill Clark. Cannon said, "At a subsequent meeting, Reagan told me how you could do everything you had to at the ranch. What you couldn't do, I said—and he conceded—was get [Secretary of State] Shultz, [Secretary of Defense] Weinberger and Clark quickly together in one room. You had to do that in Washington. For the purpose Reagan used the ranch, to recharge his batteries, it was perfect. On the other side of the coin, the isolation made it difficult for conferring in person."

THE OPEN "MIKE"

On another occasion, a facetious remark by Reagan made news. One time, during a microphone check before one of his Saturday radio broadcasts, he quipped, "My fellow Americans, I am pleased to tell you I have signed legislation to outlaw Russia forever. We begin bombing in five minutes." The press pool heard it—and reported it. Yet, this was typical Reagan. In the five years of his private-citizen daily radio commentaries, between the California governorship and the presidency, his "mike checks" always took a jocular form. This time, though, as Cannon put it, "It made quite a splash." The news-hungry media had a story for a change.

"In the story I wrote after the incident, I said that it hadn't been a wise thing to do," Cannon recalls. "In talking with Reagan about it later, he conceded the point. He kidded during microphone checks after that, but never again about the Soviet Union."

At the next radio taping, CBS's Susan Zirinsky, who accompanied the media pool, held up a sign to the president that read, "OPEN MIKE." Reagan laughed, saying, "It's not big enough for me!"

Not every press pool trip to the ranch was in balmy weather. One in particular was hair-raising. Of the trip to cover the arrival of Queen Elizabeth II and Prince Philip in February 1983, Cannon says, "There was a tremendous storm and I remember having to see Larry Speakes, the press secretary, that morning about some details, Donnie Radcliffe of the *Post* was traveling with the queen. Speakes occupied a fairly large room above the briefing room at the Sheraton. We looked outside and there was a boat floating in the parking lot. The trees were bent over as if in a hurricane. When I went with the press pool it was a frightening experience going up that road, even in four-wheel-drive vehicles.

"Spy" Cameras

With no solid news on most days, the television cameras were always looking for good visuals to pep up their nightly news broadcasts. This led the three broadcast networks to a mountainside in Los Padres National Forest, opposite the Reagan ranch. CBS White House correspondent Bill Plante says, "We poured a concrete slab to make a level platform for the camera pedestal. It may have been against Forest Service regulations, but we used it every day and it may still be there."

Zirinsky recalls, "We had a very powerful telephoto lens, one strong enough to see the space shuttle. Our engineer, Greg Amadon, developed one that was even more powerful. It was so big we had to rent a Ryder truck to carry it around in. With it we would see the president come out of the house, ride his horses, and so forth. Once we saw him come out the front door in a red bathrobe, as if looking for the morning paper. We didn't use that photo."

She adds, "One of our telephotos of him was published in the local newspaper. When Mrs. Reagan saw that she thought we had gone too far. Soon our telephoto lens picked up the sight of a curtain hanging over the bathroom window with a sign on it which seemed to read 'Just say NO'."

Each network had a crew on the mountainside throughout the

daily hours during the Reagan sojourns at Rancho del Cielo. Communications from the crews to their production bases in Santa Barbara were sophisticated. Susan Zirinsky remembers that their cameraman, Gabe Romero, devised a system "that hooked up walkie-talkies with regular telephones and signal repeaters. Until the Secret Service began scrambling their internal communications we could monitor their conversations. One time one agent said over the phone to another, 'If you see Susan Zirinsky tell her Larry Speakes [the press secretary] is looking for her.' They knew we would get the message, so I called Larry and said, 'You're looking for me?'"

THE NEWS MEDIA AS GUESTS

The Reagans held one big social event at the ranch for the press corps in pre-presidential days. On Monday, June 28, 1976, at the end of the presidential primary and state convention season—and seven weeks before the opening of the Republican National Convention in Kansas City—the Reagans invited all the media people who had been covering the primaries, plus several from the Sacramento press corps, along with Reagan's senior staff, to a barbecue at the ranch. Seventy or so guests dined at umbrella tables, savoring the cloudless day and the sights of Rancho del Cielo.

During the presidential years, the Reagans gave an annual party for the news media covering him. It was usually held at a Santa Barbara hotel, but some were held at actor Fess Parker's place in Hope Ranch, a community of large properties outside Santa Barbara. At his last Santa Barbara barbecue for the press, President Reagan announced that on leaving office, "I'm going to start working for a constitutional amendment . . . to make every president spend his vacation in Santa Barbara!"

REAGAN IN PUBLIC & PRIVATE

Reagan's press secretaries recognized that there were frequent news vacuums and tried to fill them, according to Cannon. "They would announce something or have a news event, but Reagan had far fewer of these during his ranch visits than other presidents did on their retreats. Nixon, for example, was always having 'news events' and calling his time off 'a working vacation.' Reagan never did that. He didn't feel you had to tell people you were working if you weren't."

Cannon adds, "I don't see how you can be in that job and be begrudged time away. Reagan was a private figure as well as a public one. He liked the stage, sure, but he also valued the time he wasn't on stage. It was genuine. He liked to work with his hands, liked to ride, to build fences. The TV camera 'spy' thing is interesting. He didn't particularly want to be seen doing what he was doing. Yet, from a public relations angle, those pictures were helpful to Reagan. After all, what's harmful about building fences, chopping wood, driving your Jeep? They are manly, Western things to do. Those telephoto pictures of him reinforced the positive image people had of him. Yet, he wasn't doing any of it for 'image,' but because those are the things he liked to do."

9
AFTER THE WHITE HOUSE YEARS

On January 20, 1989, with the inauguration of George Bush as President, Rancho del Cielo was no longer the "Western White House." This did not diminish its importance as a retreat for Reagan, for his next five years were filled with travel, speeches, and regular office hours to greet a constant stream of visitors. Visits to the ranch were more frequent than they had been during the White House years, for they involved only a drive from the Reagans' new home in Los Angeles.

By law, former presidents are protected for life by the Secret Service, but with a smaller detail than during presidential days. The Service's equipment and surveillance systems, installed in time for Reagan's inauguration eight years earlier, were left in place and used when the Reagans were at the ranch. Unlike the presidential years, however, the ranch did not get Secret Service protection when he was not there.

The former president's calendar shows these highlights, interspersed by visits to the ranch, ranging in duration from two to seven days:

1989. June 10–17: travel to London (where he received an honorary knighthood from Queen Elizabeth) and Paris; October 20–28: trip to Japan; November 11–16: to New York for a speech at West Point and to Washington, D.C. for the unveiling of his official White House portrait.

There were ranch visits in April, twice in May, June, August, September and December.

1990. June 3–4: meeting with Mikhail Gorbachev in San Francisco; July 21: attended the Goodwill Games in Seattle; September 9–20: travel to Berlin, Warsaw, Gdansk (at the shipyard where the Solidarity movement was born), Leningrad, and Moscow where he gave major speeches and received a hero's welcome. The final stop on the trip was Rome, where he met with the Pope; October 27–31: a trip to New York and his home town of Dixon, Illinois; December 2–8: a trip to Britain, with an address to the Cambridge Union and meeting with Queen Elizabeth, Lady Margaret Thatcher, and then-Prime Minister John Major.

Ranch visits: every month from January through July and September through November.

1991. March 25–28: a trip to New York and then to Washington, D.C., for the naming of George Washington University Hospital's emergency services unit in his honor; meetings with then-President Bush at the White House, with Dick Cheney, then Secretary of Defense, and General Colin Powell, then Chairman of the Joint Chiefs of Staff. May 17: dinner with Queen Elizabeth on the *Britannia* in Miami. October 11–21: travel to Morocco (Rabat, Fez, Bouznika, Marrakech), England, and Scotland. November 4: dedication of the Ronald Reagan Presidential Library attended by President Bush and former Presidents Carter, Ford, and Nixon.

Ranch visits: one every month of the year.

1992. May 8–10: a visit to his alma mater Eureka College, Eureka, Illinois. He went on to New York for meetings with Gorbachev and joint events at Radio City Music Hall, and the New York Stock Exchange. On August 17, he addressed the Republican National Convention in Houston. In October, he made numerous appearances for Republican candidates in California, Arizona, New Mexico, Georgia, and North Carolina. November 29–December 5: travel to London for an address to the Oxford Union, a meeting with Queen Elizabeth, and one at Number Ten Downing Street with Prime Minister John Major.

There were ranch visits in January and every month from March through December, with two in May. During one of the May visits, the Reagans were hosts to the Gorbachevs.

1993. On January 13, the Reagans journeyed to the White House, where he received the Medal of Freedom from President Bush. On May 15, he gave an address at The Citadel in South Carolina. September 22–24: a trip to New York City to receive the Intrepid Freedom Award and to have meetings with former President Nixon and South African President F. W. de Klerk.

There was a visit to Rancho del Cielo in each of the twelve months. At the ranch in February, the Reagans hosted Lady Thatcher and in April Prime Minister Brian Mulroney of Canada and his wife.

1994. February 1–4: he was in New York and Washington, where the climax of the trip was a large gathering of Republican friends and colleagues to celebrate his eighty-third birthday. Lady Thatcher spoke, as did Reagan, in what would prove to be his last address to a major political gathering. In March, he gave a speech in Palm Springs to a business group; he had given a number of talks to business and professional groups during the early years of his retirement. On April 27, he and

Mrs. Reagan attended Richard Nixon's funeral in Yorba Linda, California. On June 21, he met the Emperor and Empress of Japan. As his public schedule began to thin out, he began to enjoy longer visits to Rancho del Cielo. The Reagans spent five to seven days in each of the first eleven months of the year and three days in December.

Throughout these years ranch days were much as they had been during the White House years: horseback riding, fence mending, brush cutting, but also relaxed enjoyment of the clear air and sunny views.

On November 5, 1994, in a letter to the American people, Reagan made the stunning announcement that, "I have recently been told that I am one of the millions of Americans who will be afflicted with Alzheimer's Disease." In his two-page, handwritten letter he was typically upbeat, without a trace of self-pity. He wrote, "I intend to live the remainder of the years God gives me on this earth doing the things I have always done. I will continue to share life's journey with my beloved Nancy and my family. I plan to enjoy the great outdoors and stay in touch with my friends and supporters." As always, he was optimistic about the nation's future. He concluded with these words, "I now begin the journey that will lead me into the sunset of my life. I know that for America there will always be a bright dawn ahead. Thank you, my friends. May God always bless you."

He continued to go daily to his post-Presidential office in Los Angeles over the next few years; however, as the effects of Alzheimer's Disease gradually circumscribed his world, the ranch activities he had so enjoyed were less and less possible. He visited Rancho del Cielo for the last time in the late summer of 1995.

The Decision to Sell the Ranch

In 1997, Nancy Reagan made the wrenching decision to sell the ranch. Dennis LeBlanc, one-time aide to her husband and his co-worker during the ranch's rebuilding phase, was asked by Mrs. Reagan to be their representative at the ranch when prospective buyers visited it.

Then-Governor Pete Wilson raised the idea of the federal government underwriting purchase of the property, thence to be run—with private contributions—as a state park. The idea ran into political opposition, however, and went no further.

In April 1998, a buyer came forward. It was the Young America's Foundation, a twenty-nine-year-old non-profit organization descended from a conservative college-age group, Young Americans for Freedom (YAF), in which many "Reaganauts" had been active all the way back to the Goldwater campaign of 1964. The sale took place on April 21.

Not long afterward, Mrs. Reagan visited the ranch to return a large number of personal effects she had removed when the property went on the market. This act made it possible for those who visit it today to see the ranch house just as it was when the Reagans lived there. Other presidential sites must scramble to recover original furnishings and often must settle for replicas or items "of the period." In this case, everything in the house is authentic. Responding to the Foundation's promise to keep the ranch as they had known it, Mrs. Reagan said at the time of the sale, "It is comforting to know that the ranch we cherish will be preserved and protected in its present state."

The YAF Stewardship

As with other historic properties, Rancho del Cielo requires constant maintenance. The "Gipper" is no longer there to clear brush or mend fences. This must be done by the small ranch staff. The Young America's Foundation has carefully tended to these responsibilities. According to Marilyn Fisher, the foundation's curator for Rancho del Cielo who formerly worked at the Ronald Reagan Presidential Library, temperature and humidity must be carefully controlled in the ranch house and tack room to preserve their contents. Clothing, furniture, saddles, and vehicles all must be kept dusted, vacuumed or otherwise cleaned. Fisher and the foundation's Santa Barbara office staff are cataloging the collection of books, pictures, furniture, and decorative items.

Regular termite inspections are made and there have been repairs and updates to water, sewer, and electrical systems, but of course these are not visible to the eye.

What is very visible is the small "herd" of livestock donated by rancher-supporters of Young America's Foundation. There are now seven Longhorn steers, three horses, and a burro to graze the pasture.

The Ranch Today and Tomorrow

According to Ron Robinson, president of the Young America's Foundation, "We want to make the ranch as widely accessible as possible; however, there are limitations." County regulations permit "corporate retreats" in this rural area. In practice, this means that the foundation may take small numbers of students who attend its leadership conferences in Santa Barbara to the ranch for day visits. On occasion, the foundation has arranged to rent facilities at nearby Rancho LaScherpa, a Presbyterian camp and conference center, to house its own conferees so they could experience a full weekend of visits to Rancho del Cielo.

Currently, the foundation conducts Student Leadership Conferences of three or four days each in the spring and fall in Santa Barbara. Approximately 350 students attend these conferences. There are panel discussions and speakers. Among conference speakers have been such senior Reagan Administration "alumni" as Edwin Meese III, former U.S. Attorney General; William P. Clark, former Deputy Secretary of State, National Security Adviser, and Secretary of the Interior; Richard V. Allen, former National Security Adviser; and Reagan biographer and scholar Dinesh D'Souza.

In 2001 the foundation purchased the former Neal Hotel, near the Santa Barbara railroad station and across the street from a youth hostel. Shortly after the purchase, the foundation moved its Santa Barbara offices to the building's third floor. The second floor of the 21,000-square-foot building is being remodeled and will hold future Student Leadership Conferences. Plans are underway to make the ground floor a reception area and Reagan Ranch Museum. According to Robinson, several items from the ranch may be housed there, such as one of the Jeeps. The student conferees will be housed in the youth hostel.

During his governorship and the presidency, Reagan regularly addressed meetings of YAF. He has said, "Young America's Foundation has been a refuge for students seeking an alternative to the politically-correct environment forced on many campuses."

The foundation returns the favor in its web site description of its program, noting that the Student Leadership Program "will teach generations of students about leadership . . . the principles of freedom, limited government, and respect for traditional American values such as patriotism, courage, and personal responsibility. Young America's Foundation believes that it is Reagan's dedication to precisely these principles that made him one of the greatest presidents in our nation's history."

One purpose of the Santa Barbara conferences, according to Ranch Curator Marilyn Fisher, is that "they meet students from other parts of the country who have a similar outlook." She says that some go on to become YAF interns during summer vacation or the winter school break at the foundation's headquarters in Herndon, Virginia, outside of Washington, D.C., or at the Santa Barbara office. During the summer of 2001, there were five student interns at the Santa Barbara facility.

The twisting, narrow road to the ranch, coupled with County usage regulations restricts the number of students that can be accommodated at the ranch at a given time. Visiting groups usually consist of thirty to forty student conferees. Typically, they spend half a day visiting the ranch and have a picnic lunch. Often, John Barletta, the retired Secret Service agent, will give a talk on the shore of Lake Lucky about ranch life during the Western White House years, then conduct the group on a tour of the ranch house and barns. Says Robinson, "Rancho del Cielo is unique in its ability to illustrate the life of

President Reagan, both as a public figure and private individual. At the ranch, students see first-hand how he lived and can better understand the principles that guided his life."

OUTREACH

While the general public cannot visit the Rancho del Cielo at this time, Robinson notes that the foundation has made it accessible to the news media. C-SPAN provided extensive coverage of the ranch in its "American Presidents" episode about Reagan. FOX and CNN have also provided coverage. The foundation also maintains a web site, *www.reaganranch.org*, which has a number of color photos of the ranch.

He once called it his "open cathedral." He'd come out of the house and look at the sky and not say a word. The Great Communicator didn't talk a lot in those circumstances. Many don't understand that, but he would just look about him with that great grin.

—William P. Clark

BIBLIOGRAPHY

Index

A

Adams, Abigail, 4
Adams, John, 3–4
addresses, speaking engagements
    address supporting Goldwater, 41, 67
    at California Statehouse, 36–37
    at 1976 Republican National
        Convention, 43–44
    post-governorship, 34, 41
    post-presidency, 94–97
Adirondack Mountains, New York, 7
Allen, Richard V., 73, 100
Alta California, 16
Alzheimer's Disease, 97
Amadon, Greg, 89
An American Life (Reagan), 30–31
Anderson, Martin, 58–59, 72
Angulo, Virginia, 24
Ash Lawn, 4

B

Baker, Howard, 76
Barletta, John, 59–61
Barnett, Willard "Barney," 30, 36–38, 42,
    45, 60–61
Bazzi, Natale, 24
Bear Flag Revolt, 22–23
Berlin disco bombing, 75
birthday celebrations
    Nancy Reagan's, 29, 68
    Reagan's 83rd birthday, 96
Black Hills, South Dakota, 7, 82
Bouchard, Hippolyte de, 20–21
Britannia (Royal Yacht), wedding
    celebration on, 69–70
Brown Derby Restaurant, 37–38
Brown, Jerry, 36–37
Burroughs, John, 6
Bush, Barbara, 70
Bush, George H., 11, 70, 71, 96
Bush, George W., 12

C

Californios, 22
Camp David, 8, 9, 11
Camp Rapidan, 8
Cannon, Lou, 30–31, 71

on events involving press corps, 85,
    87–89, 91
Carter, Jimmy, 11, 71, 86
Casa Pacifica, 10
Casey, Bill, 74
Catoctin Mountains, Maryland, 8
Clark, William P., 73–75, 87, 100
Clinton, Bill, 11–12
Cobb, Sally, 37
Combetto, Margaret, 24
Coolidge, Calvin, 7, 82
Cornelius, Raymond and Rosalie, 24–25,
    29–30
Crespi, Juan, 17

D

daily life at the ranch, 71–73, 78–79
Dakota Territory ranches, 4
de Klerk, F. W., 96
de la Guerra, José, 20
"Death Valley Days" (TV show), 67
Deaver & Hannaford, 35
Deaver, Michael, 35, 41, 77, 87
Disney Corporation, 60
Donaldson, Sam, 83–84
driving, Reagan's enjoyment of, 52
D'Souza, Dinesh, 100
Duberstein, Kenneth, 76

E

Economic Recovery Act of 1981, The,
    76–77
    signing of, 86–87
Edison, Thomas, 6
Eisenhower, Dwight, 9
El Camino Real (Royal Road), 17
El Refugio canyon, 17
Elizabeth II (Queen of England), 69,
    88–89, 95
entertaining
    barbecues, for press corps, 90
    birthday celebrations, 29, 68, 96
    at LBJ Ranch, 10
    party at launch of radio talks, 37–38
    at Rancho del Cielo, 68–69
Erhard, Ludwig, 10
Eureka College, 95

F

Fages, Pedro, 16
Firestone, Harvey, 6
Fisher, Marilyn, 99
fishing, Coolidge's passion for, 7–8
Flournoy, Frank, 24
Ford, Gerald, 11, 34, 42
Ford, Henry, 6
Fremont, John C., 22
Fuess, Claude M., 82

G

Galvez, José de, 16
Gandolio, Charles and Mary, 24
"General Electric Hour, The" (TV show),
    67
Gettysburg, Pennsylvania, 9
Goggia, Arlangelo and Luigi, 24
Goldwater, Barry, Reagan's support for,
    41, 67
Gorbachev, Mikhail, 70–71, 95–96
guest accommodations
    at LBJ Ranch, 10
    at Rancho del Cielo, 39–40, 52

H

Haarlachen artists colony, 6
Haig, Alexander, 74
Harding, Florence, 6
Harding, Warren, 6–7
Heart Rock, 72
helicopters/helicopter pad, 60–61
Hill Rush, 39
Hoover, Herbert, 8
Hope Ranch, 90–91
horses, horseback riding
    daily rides, 71–73
    on first visit the ranch, 30–31
    importance of, for Reagan, 45, 59, 66,
        97
    mounted Secret Service protection,
        61–62
    pet cemetery, 53
    in Reagan's films, 28, 66
Hyannisport, Massachusetts, 9
Hyde Park, New York, 8

I

Intrepid Freedom Award, 96
intruders, at Rancho del Cielo, 62–63

J

Japan, Emperor and Empress of, 97
Jefferson, Thomas, 3, 4
John Paul II, 95
Johnson, Lady Bird, 9
Johnson, Lyndon, 9–10
Jorgenson, Earle and Marion, 68
Joslin, Ted, 8

K

Kennedy, John, 9
Key Biscayne, Florida, 10
kitchen at Rancho del Cielo, 39, 50
knighthood, honorary, 94
Korean Airlines flight 007, shooting
    down of, 74, 87

L

Laghi, Pio, 70
Lake Lucky, 40–41, 50
land concessions, by Spanish, 18
Lasuén, Fermin, 17
Law and Order (movie), 28–29
Laxalt, Paul, 69
LBJ Ranch, 9–10
LeBlanc, Dennis, 31, 36, 38, 45, 98
lectures. See addresses, speaking
    engagements
Lincoln, Abraham, 5
Lindbergh, Charles and Anne, 8
Linkletter, Art, 37
living room/dining room, at Rancho del
    Cielo, 49–50
Los Padres National Forest, 88–89

M

MacDonald, Ramsay, 8
Madison, James, 4
Major, John, 95
Marion, Ohio, 6
master bedroom at Rancho del Cielo, 51
McFarlane, Robert, 70
Medal of Freedom award, 96

media coverage, at Rancho del Cielo,
83–89
Meese, Edwin III, 68, 100
mission system, Spanish, 17–18
Monroe, James
Monterey, CA, 17, 18, 20–21
Monticello, 3–4
Montpelier, 4
Mount Vernon, 3
Mull, Karl, 53
Mulroney, Brian and Mila, 71

N

national/international events, handling
of, while at ranch, 74–77
national security briefings, 73–74
"Nature's Laboratory," Maryland, 6
Naval Station, Key West, 9
New Spain, 16
newspaper columns, by Reagan, 34, 36,
38
Nixon, Richard, 10, 91, 96, 97

O

O'Connor, Harry, 37, 77
Ortega, José Francisco de, 16, 18–19
Ortega, José Maria, 21

P

Parker, Fess, 90–91
Pass Christian, Mississippi, 6
patio, at Rancho del Cielo, 49
Peacefield, 4
Pershing, John, 6
pet cemetery at Rancho del Cielo, 53
Philadelphia, federal capitol at, 3
Philip, Duke of Edinburgh, 69
physical labor, Reagan's enjoyment of,
38–39, 40, 45, 84, 97
Pico, José Jesús and Juana, 23–24
Plains, Georgia, 11, 86
Plymouth Notch, Vermont, 7
poker, Truman's enjoyment of, 8–9
Poplar Forest, 3, 4
Portola, Gaspar de, 16–17
presidential campaign, 1976, 42, 69
presidential campaign, 1980, 58, 69

presidential retreats, historical, 4–12.
See also Rancho del Cielo
press corps, coverage of ranch activities,
82–86
open "mike" incident, 88–89
Reagan's annual parties for, 90
privateers, Argentinean, attempted inva-
sion by, 20–21

Q

Qaddafi, Muammar, 75–76
quarries, near Reagan ranch, 24

R

Radcliffe, Donnie, 89
radio announcer, Reagan's career as, 66
radio commentaries/addresses, 34
initiation and production of, 37–38
during presidency, 77–78
taping of, 86
railroad excursions, Harding's enjoyment of, 6–7
"Ranch Reports," 83
Ranchero system, 22–23
Rancheros Visitadores, 69
Rancho California, 29
Rancho del Cielo
completion of renovations, 45
daily life at, 71–73, 78–79
entertaining at, 68–69
famous visitors to, 69–71
guest accommodations, 39–40, 52
original owners, 23–25
purchase of, 31
Reagans' first visit to, 28, 30
Reagan's last visit to, 97
renovations, 38–39
sale of, to Young America's Foundation,
98
Secret Service protection at, 59–61
tour of, 48–53
visits to, after end of Presidency,
95–97
visits to, during Presidency, 11
Rancho LaScherpa, 100
Rancho Mirage, California, 11
Rancho Nuestra Senora del Refugio. *See*

Refugio Ranch,
Reagan Doctrine, 70
Reagan, Nancy
  birthday parties, 29, 68
  closeness with Ronald, 41, 68, 73
  first visit to Rancho del Cielo, 30
  furnishing of Westwood office, 34–35
  renovations to Rancho del Cielo, 39
  response to telephoto camera, 89–90
Reagan Ranch Museum, plans for, 100
Reagan, Ronald
  activities follow presidency, 94
  closeness with Nancy, 41, 68, 73
  departure from Governor's office, 34
  early career, 66
  enjoyment of driving, 52
  enjoyment of physical labor, 38–39,
    40, 45, 84, 97
  film career, 66
  post-gubernatorial activities, 34–38,
    44–45
  post-presidential activities, 94–96
  presidency of Screen Actors Guild, 67
  public service career, 67–68
  purchase of Ranch del Cielo, 25
  speech at 1976 Republican National
    Convention, 43–44
  speech in support of Goldwater, 41, 67
  television career, 67
  visits to Camp David, 9
Reagans, The: A Political Portrait
  (Hannaford), 36
Refugio Bay, 20, 21
Refugio Ranch (Rancho Nuestra Senora
  del Refugio), 18–19, 21, 23
Rennie ranch, 24
Republican National Convention (1976),
  34, 41, 42–43
Reynolds, Nancy, 36
Rishell, Robert, 51
Robinson, Ron, 99
Robles, Belisanio, 24
Romero, Gabe, 90
Romero, José Jesús, 24
Ronald Reagan Presidential Library, 31,
  71, 95
Room by room tour of Rancho del Cielo,
  49–53

Roosevelt, Franklin D., 8
Roosevelt, Theodore, 5–6

S

Sacramento, 36–37
Sadat, Anwar, 74
Sagamore Hill, 4
San Diego presidio, 16, 18
San Francisco, CA, Spanish settlement,
  17–18
Santa Barbara Biltmore, 85–86
Santa Barbara, CA, 16–18, 21–22
  press corps activities in, 85–86
Santa Barbara Channel, views of, from
  ranch, 72
Santa Barbara Sheraton Hotel, 85
Santa Ynez Valley/Mountains, 17–18, 21,
  72
Schreiber, Taft, 29
Schweicker, Richard, 43
Screen Actors Guild, 67
Seagirt, New Jersey, 6
Secret Service protection
  during 1976/1980 campaigns, 58
  code names for the Reagans, 58
  command center at ranch, 48, 53, 60
  handling of intruders, 62–63
  during horseback rides, 61–62
  following 1980 election, 59–61
  following presidency, 94
  Western Protective Division, 59
security enhancements for,
  at Rancho del Cielo, 59–60
  during post-gubernatorial period, 36
Serra, Junipero, 17
"Shangri-La". See Camp David
Shenandoah National Park, 8
Shultz, George, 76, 87
Smith, William French, 29
smuggling, 19–21
Solá, Pablo Vicente, 20–21
Soldier's Home, 5
Spanish land grants, 18
Speakes, Larry, 70, 88, 90
staff
  at presidential retreats, 6, 7, 10
  at Reagan's Westwood office, 36

stone patio, Reagan's laying of, 38
Student Leadership Program (YAF),
100–101
"Summer White House," 3–4, 5
Swampscott, Massachusetts, 7

T

tack barn at Rancho del Cielo, 52–53
telephoto cameras, 89–90
Thatcher, Margaret, 70, 95
time capsule story, 43–44
Tip Top Ranch, 24, 31
travels, Reagan's, following presidency,
94–97
Treaty of Guadalupe Hidalgo, 22
"Tru Luv" canoe, 40–41
Truman, Harry, 8–9
Truman, Margaret, 9

U

U.S. 101 (*El Camino Real*), 17

V

Vail, Colorado, 11
von Damm, Helene, 36

W

Walker's Point, 11
Warm Springs, Georgia, 8
Washington, George, 3
Washington, Martha, 3
Webb, Jack, 37
Weil Hotel, purchase of, by YAF, 100
Weinberger, Casper, 87
West Side Republican Women's Club, 36
Western Protective Division (Secret Service), 59
Western White House, 38
Westwood office, 35–36
Wilbur, Ray Lyman, 8
Williamsburg (presidential yacht), 8–9
Willis, Doug, 37
Wilson, Ellen, 6
Wilson, Pete, 98
Wilson, William and Betty, 29, 30, 68
Wilson, Woodrow, 6

Wyatt, Kenneth, 49

Y

Yearling Row Ranch, 28–29
Young America's Foundation (YAF)
care and maintenance of ranch, 99
leadership conferences, 100
purchase of Rancho del Cielo, 53, 98
purchase of Weil Hotel, 100

Z

Zirinsky, Susan, on events involving
press corps, 85–90

Front and back book covers, Rancho del Cielo Album pictures 1-7, 32-35, 38-51: Courtesy of Ronald Reagan Presidential Library

Pages 1, 13: Courtesy of Images from the Past

Rancho del Cielo Album pictures 8-13, 15, 17, 20, 27, 30, 31, 36, 37, 52: Photographer, Steve Malone, Courtesy of Young America's Foundation: The Reagan Ranch

Rancho del Cielo Album picture 14: Courtesy of the author

Rancho del Cielo Album pictures 16, 18, 19, 21-26, 28, 29: Photographer, Hal Conroy, Courtesy of Young America's Foundation: The Reagan Ranch

Ronald Reagan and His Ranch

The Quotable Calvin Coolidge

The Essential George Washington

The Quotable Ronald Reagan

Recollections of Reagan

My Heart Goes Home: A Hudson Valley Memoir

Remembering Reagan (co-author)

Talking Back to the Media

The Reagans: A Political Portrait